Poetry in Flight
POESÍA EN VUELO

Anthology in Celebration of El Tecolote

 Acción Latina

Front cover original B&W image by Juan R. Fuentes
http://juanrfuentes.com/

Anthology layout, coloring and design
by Adrian Arias.

Editors: Francisco X. Alarcon, Eva Martinez, Nina Serrano
with assistance by Harold Terezon

Poetry in Flight
POESÍA EN VUELO
Anthology in Celebration of El Tecolote

Introduction by
Juan Felipe Herrera
Poet Laureate of the United States

Editors
Francisco X. Alarcón (posthumous)
Eva Martinez
Nina Serrano
With assistance by **Harold Terezon**

ACKNOWLEDGEMENTS

The editorial committee is grateful for the support of the following people and organizations:

Juan R. Fuentes for creating the beautiful art to bless the cover of this anthology.

Francisco X. Alarcon's UC Davis graduate students: Lizeth Cruz, César Salgado and Juan Andrés Villa Manzo. We share in your sorrow over the loss of our mentor and friend.

The current and past staff of Acción Latina and El Tecolote who have kept the torch burning for 47 years plus.

Paul Richards who provided the editorial committee with delicious home cooked meals that powered us through long evening meetings.

And a very special thinks to Javier Pinzon for his support and the photograph of Francisco X. Alarcon.

Dedicated to Francisco X Alarcon, MamaCoAtl (Silvia Parra) and Alfonso Texidor

Photo of Silvia Parra MamaCoAtl by Adrian Arias

TABLE OF CONTENTS

FOREWORD

TecoPoetas from La Mission Will and Shall Continue

All I have is deep love for this El Tecolote Anthology—it has been a long, brave, flowering, organizing road of dedicated, rough-cut, changemaker poets, artists and writers without a home once upon a time—until they found their soul-roots in the offices of El Tecolote Newpaper, bilingual and revolutionary, in the Frida Kahlo flame-rising heart of La Misión. That's right. Many writers traveled this road, many decades ago.

Way before Latinx writers in The Mission, in 1887, we had the Mexican writer, Miguel Prieto who wrote *Viajes a los Estados Unidos.* Downtown, San Francisco, after visiting Chinatown and jotting the price of the dishes, he stepped into a bar, frowned and grimaced, jumped back—when he noticed a Mexicano with his chipped boots on the table, his swarthy, pocked face, prickly mustache, whiskey in hand and tilted chicharrón-shaped sombrero—an "¡Ayankado!" He said, an Americanized Brown. He was becoming aware that things were changing, that we all were changing, but was he right—Ayankado?

Another shift—perhaps more comfortable—in a classy apartment, with drinks, after signing the writer's "album," Prieto joined the "Tertullia," a Latina and Latino Bay Poet's private and polite reading. Señor Prieto sat down and listened to the poems of the day, in Spanish. More then seventy years later, in 1955, hailing from La Missión (20th and Harrison Streets) my uncle Roberto Quintana, a few years after arriving from El Paso, set up the first Mexicano Cultural festival at the Scottish Auditorium downtown, SF. That's right—with poems, dance, MC's (he had been a famous radio actor, poet and comedy star, with Tin Tan, in Juarez—for the new and booming XEJ radio station)—and music. But the Scottish Auditorium was far from The Mission. Fifteen years later, in the early seventies, or so—things started to heat up right here in the Big Mission. And even Tin Tan came back to life—in the incredible Tin Tan large format poetry, art and journal with reports from Central America, a tabloid magazine headed by Alejandro Murguía, Roberto Vargas and comrades. You could not miss it—with Rupert García's cilantro green and toro-blood red covers—as a matter of fact, just for the pleasure and honor of it, I raced to the Bon Ami Market on 16th and Mission and paid two solid pesos for my very own bonified copy. More changes were about to roll in, a few years later—San Francisco's *El Teco fluorescence* of La Palabra Latinx in the early '80s.

Guess who was the monster-thinker, volcanic editor, boundless energy dynamo that pulled us poets and artists into the Teco revolution, in addition to Juan Gonzalez and groovy staff? Yes, correct—Francisco X. Alarcón. Pancho had the bad habit of being an effervescent, magnetic innovator. We had just come back from

Mexico City, where he exploded with the nerviest idea in that boiling caldron of artists and editors—to put together the first U.S. Latinx poetry art and essay insert, *El Suplemento Literario,* for the mega-periodical, Mexico's El Excelsior Newspaper with work from writers in La Mission—a West Coast emphasis and national antennae. Pancho followed up—"Let's do a suplemento, for El Teco, what do you think?" That's all we needed to hear—and boom-bam-zaz! El Tecolote Literario emerged from the paisley, Tehuantepecan bowels of the "Ayankado and Ayankada!" Many artists, poets from La Mission published and many from Latin America. Francisco, our dear literary leader, passed away last year—now we are here, with this magnificent anthology—a tribute to him and a culmination of many generations. A long line of cantos, songs, experiments and poems.

In these poems we have "Dear Mr. President," written by Maurisa Thompson, a writer with roots in the Fillmore, in the voice of a child held in detention, making a plea to return home. A child without a home—a social being that lives in-be-tween spaces, in the penumbra waiting for authentic, unfettered citizenship—neither here nor there—in a political container, by force. Other poems speak of the streets, they shout out the recurring question of La Mission's inhabitants, "can I erase / the extranjeros building so high into the sky?" In a few words—can we stop the foreigners, the strangers, from surrounding us? From containing us, imprisoning us? And there are Griot masks, shout outs to Mission poets, like Avotcja and Texidor, Lorca-like moons, the cosmic powers of singers and poets, and Mission murals and Chi points of healing. Notice the hotel residents taking note of the quaking economic and cultural fractures, as in Cathy Arellano's poem, "Hotel Mission: Hottest Show in Town."

This is the El Tecolote Anthology, the pioneering, fiery, soulful eye of this community, keeping watch and ward on our realities, without borders—even if the border makers insist on doing their border work. This is a volume of dreams, battle, play and the magic of the people—new freedom of thought warriors, word-salseras,—checking on that odd-angled thing called "progress," on that viral tsunami of corporate, social and economic encroachment. And in its various forms the cement of such progress cannot bury that which "breaks back through stone," as Victor Martinez, one of our great and late poets, once said in his poems. Here you find the spirit of beauty, creative continuity, and transcendence. Carry this book with your life it is made of many lives.

¡¡Viva la Misión!!

Juan Felipe Herrera
Poet Laureate of the United States.

PREFACE

This anthology was planned to debut in 2010, seven years ago. That was the year El Tecolote newspaper turned 40 and in honor of this milestone Acción Latina, the non-profit publisher, sponsored a series of celebratory events.

That spring, Eva Martinez, director of Acción Latina, and Alfonso Texidor, El Tecolote's calendario editor, sent out a plea for help to honor El Tecolote's literary history. By supreme luck *la diosa de las almas buenas* sent Francisco X. Alarcon to the rescue and he set about forming an editorial committee to produce a literary supplement. Soon Eva and Alfonso were meeting regularly with local poets Nina Serrano and Estela de La Cruz under the knowledgeable guidance of Francisco.

Their first completed project was a beautiful *Revista Literaria* edition of El Tecolote, its pages filled with old school and new school poets and featuring cover art by long-time Tecolote artist, Juan R. Fuentes. The committee's next project was to be a poetry anthology, a real book to be published in late fall. But it didn't happen. Life got in the way. Pulled by busyness, new jobs and family needs we all went our separate ways with a promise that we would reconvene and get it done. A year passed. Then two turned into four. And on Christmas Day 2014 our beloved Alfonsito Texidor passed peacefully away in a room filled with love.

In grief, we reaffirmed our commitment to the anthology. In June 2015, the committee came together with Francisco, Nina, Eva and new member Harold Terezon and issued a new call for poems. Nearly 100 poets responded with more than 200 poems. We were inspired by the diversity of voices and the quality of the work all in resistance to the growing racism, sexism, xenophobia, militarization, and gentrification around us.

And then in early December Francisco was diagnosed with stomach cancer. He made his last public appearance on January 10, 2016 at Café La Boheme in the Mission district, where an adoring crowd of hundreds flowed out onto the street. Assisted by his family Francisco read his latest poem *!Viva la Vida!*

Nine days later he was gone, leaving his presence everywhere—in bookstores, on the Web, in the classroom and on the streets of the Mission—but most conspicuously in our hearts. Again, in grief, the committee faltered then recovered to carry on the work to create this anthology you hold in your hands today. If you are quiet we are sure you will hear a community of rebellious loving spirits led by Alfonso Texidor and Francisco X Alarcon within its binding.

¡Viva La Vida!

Francisco X. Alarcon (posthumous)
Eva Martinez
Nina Serrano
with assistance by Harold Terezon

El Tecolote History

El Tecolote newspaper was born at San Francisco State University following the turbulent and successful struggle to establish the nation's first ever College of Ethnic Studies. In 1969 Juan Gonzales had just earned his B.A. in journalism when he was asked to create media curriculum for the newly minted Raza Studies department. At the time Gonzales was working for the United Press International news agency where he noticed the glaring lack of diversity in the newsroom and saw how this impacted coverage of Latino communities. At best the news was shallow, mostly it was non-existent, and sometimes it was downright racist.

When Gonzales was hired to teach the media classes he decided to improve coverage by encouraging more Latinos to enter the profession. His classroom became a newsroom that produced El Tecolote newspaper and the first issue hit the streets on August 24, 1970. The newspaper soon moved to the Mission District and became a training ground for residents interested in advocacy journalism. The staff was a collective composed of college students and community activists who discussed and argued over the principles of the budding community media outlet. They agreed that the newspaper should be bilingual in order to be accessible by everyone. They established policies that said no to advertising from tobacco, alcohol and corporations who had financial ties to oppressive oligarchies in Latin America. And they created a newsroom that became a training ground, welcoming anyone who found their way to their door.

The community supported El Tecolote. Businesses and non-profit agencies provided office space and gave donations for fundraisers. The 100 percent volunteer staff ranged from teenagers to grandparents who translated, reported, took photographs, copy edited, did layout, and jumped in and out of their cars to deliver the newspaper. In no time a new generation of community journalists was born.

In the 1980s a group of literary writers came on board to create the Revista Literaria de El Tecolote, a quarterly supplement that played an important role in giving exposure to Latino writers and cultural institutions. The editorial board included poet Francisco X. Alarcon, playwright Carlos Morton, graphic artist Sue Martínez, and poet/writer/muralist José Antonio Burciaga.

For a period of time El Tecolote's newsroom was nomadic, moving from office, to someone's garage to storefront. Wherever it landed it was the happening place where political dialogue occurred, people fell in and out love, and disagreements were argued over. People followed the owl as it soared over la Misión and beyond. El Tecolote's coverage had a real impact. It exposed the dangerous lack of Spanish language medical interpreters at San Francisco General Hospital and the absence of bilingual emergency operators at the phone company, which resulted in slower response times for Spanish-speaking people in crisis. Combined with community action, the coverage resulted in real change.

Actually nobody, including Juan Gonzales, thought that the newspaper would last past five years or so. And yet it did. Certainly there have been lean and hard years where pages were cut, it published less frequently and volunteers became scant. But over the long run El Tecolote has not simply survived, it has thrived.

Established by people who saw a need—the lack of news coverage that accurately portrayed the complexities of Latino life and culture—and who passionately gave their skills, time and money to accomplish their vision El Tecolote truly was by and for the people.

Today, El Tecolote is a trusted and effective pipeline to the media profession as it continues to train the next generation of journalists through community outreach and long-term internship collaborations with SFSU and CCSF. In addition to the online site at www.eltecolote.org the staff continues to produce a newspaper to overcome the digital divide. Every two weeks 10,000 free copies are distributed to 350 locations in the Bay Area.

In reality the staff has been producing two newspapers by staying true to its bilingual format. The extensive extra work involved, including hours spent arguing over the best phrase to use to describe complex community issues, is a testament to El Tecolote's commitment to language equality. Where many others have tried and failed, El Tecolote has successfully managed bilingualism.

For 46 years El Tecolote has served as a community eyewitness chronicling evidence of Latino economic, social and cultural contributions to San Francisco. Recently El Tecolote's newspaper and photographic archive was appraised by Libros Latinos, which stated: "The history of Acción Latina and its newspaper, El Tecolote, comprises the history of the social struggles and artistic movements of San Francisco's Mission District in particular, and of San Francisco in general, from 1970 to the present. No other existing archive contains the wealth of materials that helped precipitate, define, and describe those struggles and movements for almost half a century."

Acción Latina, the publisher of El Tecolote, was established in 1987 with a mission to promote cultural arts, community media and civic engagement as a way of building healthy and empowered Latino communities. In 2000, Acción Latina purchased a building in the heart of the Mission District at 2958 24th Street, providing a permanent home for El Tecolote and its other projects.

¡Que viva El Tecolote!

69 poems
by 56 poets

Magic Mission Flats
by Francisco X. Alarcón

among the six buildings
bought by two non-profits
in San Francisco in 2015

to keep artists from
being evicted from
their apartments

is an old house converted
into four units on San Jose
Avenue in La Misión

the two story magic
building where I dwelled
in the early 1980's together

with Chicano artists
Yolanda López, René Yáñez
and son Río Yáñez

in the second floor
front apartment with
a Samoan family inhabiting

the first floor front unit
and with Juan Felipe Herrera
-now US Poet Laureate-

his wife Margarita Robles
Luna and familia sharing
the first floor back flat

if these walls could speak
they would tell the stories
behind so many artworks

the walls would recite poems
from the many poetry books
and chapbooks written here

so many embraces, kisses
birthday parties, long chats
tasty dinners and wine toasts

here Chicano teatrista/poet/
activist Rodrigo Reyes laid
on his bed surrounded

by thirteen of his friends
before being taken away
an evening under a full moon

these are the Mission flats where
artists Yolanda López, René Yáñez
and partner Cynthia Wallis

resisted their uncalled for
evictions, led a community
movement against evictions

that are changing the face,
the heart and the soul of
the Latino Mission District

and finally won a permanent
retrieve - their Mission flats
will remain their sweet homes

Nuevo angel de la Misión
por Francisco X. Alarcón

hoy
el último día
del año

hace viento
muy oscuro
muy frío

esta noche
la Misión
se ve tan vacía

corro y entro
a La Bohéme,
pido un café latte

de repente
veo sentado
en un rincón

al Nuevo
angel radiante
de La Misión

un angel poeta
revolucionario
puertorriqueño

dedicado
a derribar fronteras
y a publicar

El Tecolote –
el periódico
de la comunidad

es Alfonso
Texidor sonriendo
a sus anchas

como el Gran Gato
de Alicia en el País
de las Maravillas

Alfonso levanta
su copa llena
de vino

y dice bien fuerte
para que todos oigan:
"¡a cortar caña!"

New Angel of the Mission
By Francisco X. Alarcon

today
the last day
of the year

it's so windy
so gloomy
so cold

tonight
The Mission
looks so empty

I run into
La Bohéme,
order a café latte

suddenly
I see seated
in a corner

the radiant
new angel
of The Mission

revolutionary
Puerto Rican
poet angel

dedicated
to tear down
borders and publish

El Tecolote –
the newspaper
of the community

it's Alfonso
Texidor smiling
as broad

as the Fat
Cat in Alice in
Wonderland

Alfonso raises
his cup full
of wine

and says aloud
for all to hear
"¡a cortar caña!"

Cantaloupe Canvas
By Amalia Alvarez

Con amor for Alex Nieto,
con justicia and bold base for Alex Nieto, with sweet, angry
trumpets blowing for Oscar Grant, and Idriss Stelly, Andy Lopez,
Michael Brown, Eric Garner, Walter Scott, Trayvon Martin and
all the black and brown men shot down in cold blood a las
manos de la policía.

There are tones of blood soaked blues and
        uniform behavior– enforcers of Jim Crow and Juan Crow

        One heart/el corazón de la missión
Chin pointed to the sun
        cruising with gold, ferris wheel rims

And Tupac sings, "Hail Mary can you hear me?"

Momentarily

I realize I am in charge of my journey
Wet earth sprouts a Cal Tjader marimba

Went to bed with a smile on my face and a full heart in my chest
Woke up to step up and get on Dr. Cornel West's "caravan of love"

Ready to tell the truth about white supremacy and the
"Plight of Black people in America"

And so I did today in class and put forth the words, and questions
in the kiva of the classroom with my open-hearted students

A bird began to call out in repetitive pattern
Earlier I thought I could hear someone breathing through the wall

Estaban los pajaritos afuera
Their voices hum without fear

Somewhere above the fog,
fireflies flutter in the midnight sky

I find myself, both in my body and in the collective
It's life force and beauty, but I also need to be alone

in my room, in my bed under the covers dreaming
awake or dreaming asleep in consciousness.

My Own Louie
By Paul Aponte

Andábamos en su ranfla
down Capitol Avenue.
You know, Capitol Avenue en SanJo.

Way Before some güey
decided to express it
by demolishing cantones
and turning it all
into a cesspool
of boiling concrete & cars.

Anyway,
Andábamos en su ranfla
down Capitol Avenue.
El Louie was driving Dad's
46 Plymouth Coupe
From Story Rd
down Capitol Avenue
approaching el Payless.
Payless:
with the huge drive-in type parking lot
where jainas and vatos hung out at night,
listened to "Angel Baby" and "Hanky Panky".

but right now it was daytime,
and two of his buddies
con su ranfla chingona
came up right next to his window.

With lip-bobbing cigarette he said:
"Ey, Louie, you got a match?"
"Órale. Hold on.
Poly, drive the car."
"¿Qué?"
"Just grab the steering wheel!"
El Louie sat on the window sil
paper matches in hand
lit up three together to make sure,
lit the vatos trola,

and sat down
before the carrucha
complained
about the 8 year old steering it.

He gave me a couple of looks
and on the 2nd gave me his signature laugh:
"Puh-th-th-thuh".
He drove me to Mark's Hot Dogs,
the place with the juiciest,
crispiest and most delicious dogs,
making me feel welcome again.

My summer vacation from el Defe,
starting off pretty well.

He'd been there himself.
Got a tough guy reputation
in a place filled with the toughest.
Constantly came back to our Tlatelolco apartment
beat up for taking on too many at once.
I imagine they called him el Tlate-loco.
So the uncles had to send him back to SanJo.

I never saw any meanness.
I only saw crazy funny,
or quiet, wistful, pensive Louie.
Though, most times he was out and about.

Even so, I do have some memories.
Like that hot summer night
when he was stuck at home for some reason.
He gave me a note, and instructions:
"All you have to do is knock on the window.
When Sylvia opens it, tell her Louie sends this.
Now, go!"
I knock. Sylvia opens the window and
immediately grabs the note without asking
and tells me to wait.
She comes back out with her thick eye-liner,
and puffy hair with the flipped out ends

and straight cut bangs barely above her brows.
She gives me another note to give to Louie.
Then I become a ping-pong ball on the
table of grounded teenagers.
I know at some point it stopped,
but I actually don't remember that moment.
I think the ghost of me or parallel universe me
is still out there doing it.

He was definitely the ladies man,
and even though he was tall & studly,
with light skin & light blue eyes,
he liked them gorditas, prietitas y bien Chicanas.
Le gustaba la guitarra just like Dad,
and he impressed the ladies just like Dad.

The summer was over.
Back en el Defe things began boiling.
Just like everywhere around the world and the U.S.

1968 came around - a horrific year.
The beginning of the Tet Offensive in Vietnam.
Labor strikes and riots in Poland, France & Italy.
Race riots throughout the U.S.
President Johnson refused to run for re-election.
Martin Luther King - assassinated.
Bobby Kennedy - assassinated.
Student riots in Mexico City.
Estudiantes contra granaderos.
In Tlatelolco where I lived -- many students were murdered.
and in 1968 ...
Mi carnal Louie died. He was 18.
He died March 30th, 1968.

The newspaper said he drowned in Coyote lake.
Maybe he drowned in sorrow
after his good friend
committed suicide.
Maybe he abused his body
and just couldn't come back out.
Maybe, as they say, he was involved with gangs

and was killed when he chose to lead a different gang,
beaten up and thrown in the water
at a supposed "going away" party.

Don't want to know.

Years after:
My sister's daughter was born ... on March 30th.
My son was born ... on March 30th.
There is a supernatural feeling about that.

I think it was 1970
cuando me retaché a mi dulce hogar
for the summer.
I remember getting a high fever, almost delirious.
In the depths of my illness
I actually felt myself feeling like I might die.
Casi estiraba el teni.
Then I had a dream.
I was in the middle of the main road
in a typical western town of the old wild west.
A strange town, unknown to me,
deserted dirt streets
and rolling tumbleweeds.
I realized I was going to be in a gun fight.
The other guy showed up at a long distance
on this main town road
in a hero's style cowboy outfit
with a red scarf blowing in the wind
I knew it wasn't my town.
I knew this man meant business
and I had no business being there.
His arms slightly out, hands wide open by the holsters.
Then I saw it was Louie.
His message was "this town, his town, ain't big enough for the both of us."

After I recuperated from my fever,
and was playing outside on a windy day,
I thought I heard in the wind his signature laugh.
"Puh-th-th-thuh."

Hotel Mission: Hottest Show in Town
By Cathy Arellano

flames
spark
spike
singe
gobble
swallow
devour

                                        smoke climbs
                    an invisible
circular staircase

hands cover frozen mouths
wide eyes close then open hoping for hope
residents - tenants start to survey their losses

his blank checks
that are useless
29 days out of the month

her photos of family
who she left long ago
or they left her
even longer

lose count
start over
again

they dream for that morning's last place position
where at least they had a place to sleep

they scoop mail
from a grimy puddle
called temporary shelter

the owner who threatened to sell each time
there was a leaky faucet
          rat or roach invasion
                    rickety staircase
complaint

has been counting his projected profits
since the last boom
makes a quick call to a contractor
hangs up with a "Hot damn!"

it's just how it goes
on hot days
in a hot market
in a hot city.

Barrio la Misión
Por Jorge Argueta

Llegué de El Salvador
Al Barrio La Misión
Mi corazón
Aquí volvió
A conocer la alegría

En el Barrio La Misión
Encontré amigos
Que en El Salvador
Ya no exsistían

En las calles de La Misión
Los volví a encontrar
Son de otros países
Tienen otros nombres
Pero son ellos
Mis amigos
Mis hermanos
Mis hermanas

Ahora todos viven
En este barrio
En esta Misión
Que todos queremos
Como a un país lejano

En el barrio La Misión
Se volvió paleta
De coco
De tamarindo
O pan de dulce
La tristeza

La nostalgia
La calman los burritos
De las taquerías
Cargan en su panza y en su lomo
Montañas, mariachis, y soles
Y vientos de pueblos y ciudades

Que ya no están tan lejos

En el Barrio La Misión
Volví a comer
Pupusas revueltas de esperanzas
Pupusas revueltas de caricias

Aquí los murales
Son espejos recordándonos
De donde venimos
Y los danzantes Aztecas
Son guerreros que nos recuerdan
Quienes somos

Aquí en la calle 24
Me paro a ver casas
Donde habita gente
Que se niega a dejar de hablar
En nahuatl, zental
Maya, quiche, o español
Gente dulce del Barrio La Misión
Que nunca para de luchar
Ni de cantar
Por la vida

Mission Neighborhood
By Jorge Argueta

I arrived
From El Salvador
To the Mission Neighborhood
Here my heart met happiness again

In this neighborhood
I found friends
That in El Salvador
Were gone

On the Mission streets
I found them again
They had different nationalities
And different names
But they are
My friends
My brothers
My sisters

They all live
Here now
In this Mission
I love as I love
My far away country

In the Mission
Sadness turned into
A coconut
A tamarind popsicle
Or sweet bread

In the taquerías
Burritos carry
In their bellies and backs
Mountains, Mariachis songs and suns
Of cities and towns
That are no longer too far away

In the Mission Neighborhood
I again ate pupusas mixed
With tenderness and hope

Here in the Mission Neighborhood
The murals are mirrors
That remind us who we are
And the Aztec dancers
Are warriors who remind us
Where we came from

Here on 24th Street
I stop to see houses

Inhabited by people
That won't give up
Speaking in Nahuatl, Zental,
Maya, Quiche, or in Spanish
Sweet people
Of the Mission Neighborhood
Who never stop singing
And never give up the struggle
For life.

Naufragios y rescates
Por Adrian Arias

I

La lluvia que espero
la raíz que se levanta
se abre mi pecho
en tu distancia
se rompe el hechizo
que encadenaba nuestras miradas
comienza el viaje.

II

He tejido un poema
con los hilos de tu mirada
un poema que abriga mi cuerpo cuando duermo
una embarcación de ilusiones
un barquito de papel
con la ausencia de tus manos
las que un día llegarán a mi rostro
sin aviso.

III

Los besos no se dibujan
se tejen
entre las sombras
se escalan
ellos van tranquilos
por el desfiladero de la piel se alzan
brincan se esparcen se detienen
porque están todos unidos
en la invisible línea del deseo.

Los hijos del cemento
Por Avotcja

Por primera vez
Cuando lloraban mis hijos
Mis preciosos
Con sus chillidos tan terribles
Y yo..... con ná ni ná
Nada mas que mi amar
¡Aiiiii..... que pena!
Solo sabra Dios que pena me dió
Mi pobreza y mis debilidades
¡Que impotencia!
Me dió un gran dolor
Una gran pena,
Una gran pena llena de mi tristeza
Sus llantos hambrientos
Cayendo en oídos sordos
En este mundo de cemento armado
Un mundo sin corazón
Sin sentimiento
Nada mas que el llorar de mis hijos
Con sus llantos tan terríbles
¡Estaba celoso el terremoto!

En éstos dias
En este mundo sofisticado
Lleno de cemento armado
Y riquezas incontables
Casas solariegas
Limosinas sin fin
Cuando lloran mis hijos
Mis hijos..... armados
Como el cemento
No hay un llanto
Un grito
O una lágrima
Ni un sonido
Solo un silencio cubierto de hielo
Y tiembla la tierra entera
Por miedo

Concrete Children
By Avotcja

When my children cried the first time
My precious babies...
They screamed so damn loud
And I..... with less than nothing
Had nothing but my loving
Mmmm, mmm, mm..... It hurt!!
Only God knows how much it hurt!
My poverty & helplessness
My impotence
Caused me pain ... great pain
A whole lot of pain full of sadness
Their hungry crying
Falling on deaf ears
In this world of reinforced concrete
This world with no heart
Without feeling
Only the crying of my children
Who screamed so loud
Even the earthquake was jealous!

In these days
In this sophisticated world
Full of hardened concrete
And uncountable riches
Ancestral mansions
And limousines without end
When my children cry
My children..... armed
Like the concrete
There is no weeping
No screaming
Or even a tear
Not a sound
Only an icy silence
And the whole Earth trembles
In fear!!!

The Dance of the Grandmothers
By Devreaux Baker

This morning I danced the Grandmothers' dance
I stamped the floorboards until they sang
I clapped my hands until the red ribbons
Fell out of night's braid and her hair flowed like water

This morning I danced wherever my feet wanted to go
I danced across the street and into the neighbor's house
I woke everyone up and yelled out I was dancing
the Grandmothers' dance and get out of my way

This morning I was like a song that carves its way
So deep in your heart it becomes you
It is your totem, your animal, telling you
How to walk, how to run, how to be a person
In this strange world

This morning I danced a dance that set us free
Out of the arms of the past and into the legs of the future
I was dancing so hard trees thought I was wind
Water thought I was light

This morning I danced the Grandmothers' dance
To wake up sorrow and say time to change tears
Into a song that spills out of your heart
Like a river of letting go

I called in all the old women and said let's wake
Everyone up, let's cause a disturbance in the air
Let's rattle the bones and throw down the dice
Of our lives and create something new

I danced this dance with bare feet and
Green gourds, with all the young ones
And all the old ones so together we
Formed one whirling shape, one dream
In this time and in this place

LOVE THE FAG IN YOU
By Denise Benavides

there is a plate
of food
in front of me,
a chair
i sit in
hurled over
and a mother
across a table
explaining
the hate she has
for the fag in me

i tell her, smug

you are the fag in me

as she wades in a dull pain
bloated

stagnant/thighed

her body is embodied in mine—
her body is embodied in mine.

i want to pickle her
in rosewater—

in the love that does not tender
its shoulders to me

the one
that leaves me
short sided

between
what is left

and

the barely
audible
distance between
her and i.

i am already forgetting
what is even left

between
her
and i.

How to Make Tamales
By Ariana Brown

Bend the sky into
a cup you can clean &
drink from; fill it
with hojas; soak
the skins, soft,
like your mother's
hands before she had
you. Bring the clear
husks to the table;
spoon the masa like
a crude painting over
newspaper & wait
to lump the cooked meats
into small gifts in
the center.

Fold,
cook,
& repeat.

Eat the hardened clouds
with your sunset mouth
& call it Christmas.
Tie rainbows on presents
& serve with Kool-aid,
iced tea, or beer, depending
on the age of the recipient.

Freeze the leftovers
& have private holidays
when the grocery money's
gone. Play your favorite
song & heat up a plate.
This is how we pray.

Elena
By Jose Hector Cadena

"Gracias Dios, gracias por darnos un lugar donde vivir"
Elena was thankful for a home, her two children grew there
near the park, near the school, near the lady who took care of them,
Teresa was her name, until Teresa found herself un
rinconcito en el cielo, and from afar Teresa could see how,
inevitably, Elena and her children were under watch by
folks who only cared about finances, money-money, and
in the the middle of the night a fire grew and the crowd cried
¿Como paso esto? How? Why? and their Mission hearts cracked
as the smoke cleared and as daylight came Elena knew she had
to be strong for her children, be strong for her community while
in the corner of the block, Elena's memories had turned charcoal,
orando Elena *estaba* when she heard a little voice behind her,
"No more evictions Elena, fight against this,". . . it was Teresa.

Refugees…Not Illegals!!!
By Christopher Carmona

clap clap clap

a journey of a thousand steps begins with a single atrocity
gang initiate   kill father/brother/mother   now you are one of us
tattoo name   on face   choices vanished/taken   like hymens in the desert
random kidnappings   kill kill kill   America needs its drugs
nations destabilized   profit profit profit   only choice   sell everything
                                                     for a single hope

clap clap clap

a journey of a single step begins with a thousand atrocities
a thousand guns a single ignorance leads to war   against starving children
locked in cages   like animals   lights always on shoe laces taken
always kept cold kills the smell   no blankets   pesticides keep them warm
dropped at bus station   no belongings   taken by ICE
only papers   that allow   access to country

clap clap clap

a journey of a thousand atrocities begins with a single ignorance
refugees not illegals   fleeing gang war torn country risked it all
refugees not illegals   rape is imminent   fathers can't protect
refugees not illegals   sons with guns to head   husbands can't protect
refugees not illegals   wife/daughter/sister/mother   can't protect

clap clap clap

a journey of a single atrocity begins with a thousand ignorances

guns guns guns   soldiers/fences/national guard   protect us from sense of
                                                                              safety
patriots patriots patriots   bring your guns and your hate   protect us from the inno-
                                                                    cent and the desperate
policy policy policy   politicians/pundits/photo ops   bring teddy bears/soccer
                                                                    balls/and plastic faces
tweet tweet tweet   send them back   they do not belong   dangerous and
                                                                              diseased

celebrities celebrities celebrities   no one on site   just Glenn Beck   cooking for
                                                                              no refugees
no Sean Penns no Eva Longorias   no Edward James Olmos' no George Clooneys
not even an Angelina Jolie   to buy Latino kid   to complete her kids from around
                                                        the world collection
guess, not far enough away   not fashionable enough   to fake concern
                                                               to fake volunteer

clap clap clap

a single shower   a hot meal   a new change of
                                                            clothes
cleanses the soul   like a thousand masses with bent knees   ever could
priest in detention center prays over children reminds them/reminds us
they are still human beings

clap clap clap

a thousand hearts   countless hours   no need for compensation
families knowing only cruelty   met with hugs/crayons/and sandwiches
a journey of a single smile begins with a thousand compassions

clap clap clap

***every time a new refugee family walks through the doors at Sacred Heart (the
refugee center in McAllen TX), all of the volunteers stop what they are doing and
clap to commemorate their arriving at a safe space***

Did You Hear What They Said?
By Lorna Dee Cervantes

after Gil Scott Heron,
for Nestora Salgado & for those who fast

They said another mother's dead,
dead and can't be buried. 43 children
disappeared after capture. Another mother
cries for half a millennium in the desert
searching for her daughter's daughter
(the deserts of our country, the only crop
remaining.) Hear what the mothers are saying.
They are Constitution bound. They are found
as the many remains in a waste, an arroyo.
Fill the heart with what another mother
is saying. Rise up in unison, a voice
for the chorus of peace. Another wave
is added to the saving waters. Here,
in Anahuac, The Place Between Two Great
Waters, all of the unburied join in. Feast,
sing between the weeping. Did you hear
what they are saying? Women and children first.

What Is A Chicana?
By Lorna Dee Cervantes

To be a Chicana is to be
a mongrel, half-breed, centipede
with a hundred avenues to bear;
To be a Chicana is to cross the street
when either side arrives times quanta,
is to dodge the anyway and never have
a home; to be a Chicana is to never speak,
never spoken to you swear on your
mother's side and then, besides your
father was... (and they decide);
To be a Chicana is to take the risk:
exposure, suicide, an uncounted number…
You maid around in an invisible suit;
You know the bite of dogs, threat of suits,
the laws—miscegenation applies to you,
who you love may not love you back; you take
The Paperbag Test and fail; you know how
to fold a bag, tie a knot in plastic; "Savage Wench"
is what they call you in the census books: to be
a Chicana is to have no category, no one
that applies; to be a Chicana
is to have a placenta in the ground over and over
in this liberty one for all here: this world
"Between Two Waters," this America here,
over and over and over 'til the age
our ancestors first engraved upon the shells
of food now gone extinct (as we were once declared),
our mothers' names erased… To be a Chicana
is be América, America, not a "race" ("…for I, too,
am America!"); Sometimes I spell it with an X:
The people (and I) birth in any language.

12/9/14
In honor of the courageous students of Arizona and the ones who would EDUCATE
and intended to be read in my and my father's place of birth, San Francisco, at the
hearing for Ethnic Studies in the case of Arizona banning books by Chicana and
other authors.

No Espanish Here
By Iris De Anda

Aquí no se habla español

se habla guanaca tapatía
lengua mestiza
se habla de noche día
se habla rápido despacio
se habla alegría tristeza
se habla revolución caminando
se habla ruido cantos
cuántas maneras de contar la vida
se habla besos abrazos
desnudo y cansado
corriendo y bailando

Aquí no se habla español

se habla tacos y pupusas
se sueña luna
se camina sol

Here we don't speak spanish

we speak guanaca tapatía
mestiza tongue
we speak night day
we speak fast slowly
we speak joy sadness
we speak revolution walking
we speak noise song
how many ways to tell of life
we speak kisses hugs
naked and tired
running and dancing

Here we don't speak spanish

we speak tacos and pupusas
we dream moon
we walk sun.

Alive at Lampedusa
By Leticia Del Toro

On radio news, breaking news of drowning at Lampedusa
It is not a name I know, but sound bites of *Italian coast*
Roman mayor, deadly seas, bring to mind so many
other refugee ships … I'm thinking of Elián,
I'm thinking of Cuba, of Ceuta and death by water
or death by desert, which is more inhumane?
Why does this report break my heart today?
Is it the exotic port name? Or the thought of Eritrean
souls downed in the Mediterranean? I once saw Euro
tourists ferried with cars to islands of sumptuous beauty
Corsica, Sardinia, Sicily, playgrounds for europeos
now haunted by Yemeya´s children
I am the daughter of a man who at age fourteen
walked the desert for days, sunsick and weakened.
He took blows to the head, then woke up in jail
to witness the broomstick beating of an elderly man.
When my father died at seventy-seven,
his house was empty, except for a Bible,
a typewriter, and notes of his own crossing at Yuma.
I have strolled on Corsican beaches and know the summer
throngs along the Côte d'Azur; what is that luxury worth?
Will we not see their faces in the waves?
Where does nationality go when the body disappears?
They are fellow citizens of my
paisas in the desert, the unnamed but numbered,
How is it that we house the dead in modern stateside morgues
but we cannot shelter the living, we cannot offer a hand?
When a child suckling his or her mother's milk empties
the right breast, does she not move on to the left?
Are we not free to search our Madre Tierra?
As free to search and settle in her fertile curves?
Refugees who'd survived the fire on the waters
did not stay put in their shelters, in spite of
welcome kits of deodorant and toothpaste.
Officials were astounded by those who fled.
To run free is to know you're hunted,
but what is worse? Death by drowning on a fiery ship
or death by heat and fortified funneling through

a hell of bracken fields and barren waste that ends in Pima county?
To be alive at Lampedusa, or Ceuta or Arizona
could only hold a lamplight to your heart.
You would know the gift of a new day, a drink of water
of refuge from the sun. For those of us settled,
what can we give in this vast land grab that is our lives,
mired in property deeds and purchasing power?
We will never know the force of hunger or the urge to run
or the absolute gold that is every day of strength and life before you.

My Mother's Word
By Mario Escobar

Amid the weary fight
when guns released their anxiety
my mother hunched her back and leaped a century
She disappeared into the purple horizon of time
leaving behind a child
leaving behind faces crushed by the rain
leaving behind the wrath of the Cadejo's claws

She gave me a kiss and told me that grandpa
would protect me from the serpent's fangs
seeking the nutritious blood of innocence
when the night mirrors the velvet color of flesh

At first I was upset
I was left alone in a world of red lines
everyday dodging headless bodies
while she was too busy running across borders

Soon she became a stranger
Six year old tears made her guilty
for traveling in the violent flow
of dreams

For many years I thought that dreams
pay no attention to a child's throbbing heart
when demons sharpen their horns
upon the bones of innocent souls

In 1989 mother came back for me
I was no longer part of her placenta

Momma, I've seen my grandmother get killed
and I know the sound of an A-37 Dragonfly
pulsing under the skin
Momma, I've seen my cousins get killed
and I know the vibrations of an M-16
breathing inside my veins
And momma…

I cried in the blanket of her arms
underneath the sugarcane of her face
while she gave me the candle of her word:

Don't forget to love humanity even when the poisonous beast
has left his mark of teeth on the skin
of your childhood.

My Mother's Bags
By Mario Escobar

My mother has two bags
full of mysteries
and like many Salvadoran women
she is very protective of her bags

As a child I was never capable of breaking
the Morse Code that came out of her bags
one day
while the past had stationed
in her lips
I was able to see what she had in her bags

In her first bag
she carries red steps
the desire of a gentle touch
scars of lonely nights
permanent blisters
the punch of a man
unwanted sex
unwanted charges
broken windows
locked doors
trembling hopes

In her second bag
she carries schizophrenic thoughts
war tears
the silhouette of a tropical night
forgotten dreams
violent lovers
painful farewells
salon kisses
dried flowers
suicide attempts
and the rhythm
of a Quixote
she calls son.

Yes, my mother has two bags
beneath her eyes.

Insomnia
By Odilia Galván Rodríguez

for Angel

it was dark almost
light and I was looking
on your side of the bed
it was empty again
I thought I'm dreaming
but not knowing really

you're lost someplace between
here and there and I keep
dreaming you back in bed
on my side where you love
to sleep when I'm gone long
but no you aren't really

you're sitting up someplace
asleep your head bobbing
back until it almost
hits the wall behind you
but then you wake yourself
either from the snoring

or from the thought it's time
to get back on that bird
and fly south far into
the greenest green there is
a jungle wide and jade
the beds there are hammocks

tied up to giant trees
en el Amazonas
or closer to it than
here where air is lighter
but I want to breathe the
jade air with you holding

me in those arms so sure
I miss you seeing me

the real one I say don't
exist she ran and joined
the circus and I hate
clowns they are really masked

killers or close to it
mad or wicked or worse
you know the kind that smile
in your face while twisting
the knife that is not sharp
enough to kill quickly

I don't want a slow death
those don't run in my tree
the family likes to make its
mind up and just do it
go or die whatever
comes first water or guns

a few have chosen guns
but most have gone water
or in their sleep but then
some woke up and had bad
nightmares of dying with
no say in the matter

where are you sleeping now
what chair in what airport
cradles your hunched body
will you miss that next plane
scheduled to fly over
the Patagonia

I send you a green kiss
wear it like a shamrock
for luck or love or for
safe journeying back home
to me in my hammock
or lying on your side.

Zapata y Frida
By Nancy Aidé González

I
By chance they meet at a bar
she drinks tequila shots
she wants to be life itself
he caresses his gun
he longs for uprising.

II
He strokes his mustache, his wet lips glistening
she touches her brow, her eyes aflame
they speak of monkeys and flowers, of war and borders
in the corner they become the world itself, spinning off axis
they laugh loudly and don't notice people staring
"Take me away," she says.

III
She places her hands on his face
studies his indigenous features
examines his eyes
"I know you," she says. "I have known you all my life.
You will cause my slow death."

IV
She unbraids her hair
her pink ribbons fall to the tierra
he take off her embroidered dress
he places his hands upon her small breasts
they devour each other's skin
thrusting and precise piercing
moaning until night melts into brightness
there are no promises made
upon the wet grass.

After she places her head upon his chest
and hears the drum of his heart
"You will remember me," she says.

V
They ride horses through Morelos
near sugar cane fields
"It is better to die on your feet than live on your knees," he says.
"Death knocks at my door," she says.
"I have no mercy," he says.
"Please have mercy on me," she says.

VI
The next time they make love
she unhinges him
touches the wilderness with abandon

hunger drives them deeper into
the topography of vermillion desire.

VII
An eagle sits on a cactus
and watches them dance to corridos
she pulls him close with her rebozo
"We are home," she says.

VIII
That night she has a dream
she is in the forest alone
she is a deer and arrows puncture her flesh
she awakes sobbing and gasping
paint splattered on her face

She reaches for him.
"No llores," he says.
"I want to be your soldadera," she says.

IX
He vanishes in the middle of the night
he leaves her a riffle with a rose in the barrel
she takes her brush and paints.

La luna llena llama
por Rafael Jesús González

>> a los inocentes
>> muertos por la policía

La luna llena llama
a los enamorados
que deleitan en su luz
y se dice que también llama
a los hombres lobos y los vampiros.
Es cierto de los enamorados
>> (siempre he sido de ellos.)
No sé de hombres-lobos y vampiros;
>> viven entre nosotros —
son los más allá de la ley
>> que matan a inocentes
dizque en nombre de la ley.
>> No necesitan de la luna.

The Full Moon Calls
by Rafael Jesús González

>> to the innocent
>> killed by police

The full moon calls
those in love
who delight in its light
& it is said it also calls
the werewolves & vampires.
It is true of those in love
>> (I have always been of them.)
I know not of were-wolves & vampires;
>> they live among us —
it is those beyond the law
>> who kill the innocent
supposedly in the name of the law.
>> They have no need of the moon.

Toda una vida
por Rafael Jesús González

Cuando uno baila con el Viejo Coyote
se compromete a la flor y al canto;
se gasta una vida con la moneda
de la palabra florida.
Allí dicen se encuentran
lo negro y lo rojo, lo arraigado,
la verdad. ¿Quién sabe?
Se vive una vida y si su flor y canto
toma raíz en los corazones
                 es vida bien gastada.

(Siendo otorgado un premio a toda una vida por la Ciudad de Berkeley,
13º Festival Anual de Poesía Berkeley, 6 de mayo del 2015)

A Whole Life
by Rafael Jesús González

When one dances with Old Coyote
one commits to flower & song;
a life is spent with the coin
of the flowering word.
There they say meet
the black & the red, the rooted,
truth. Who knows?
A life is lived & if its flower & song
takes root in hearts
                 it is a life well spent.

(On being honored with a Lifetime Achievement Award by the City of Berkeley,
13th Annual Berkeley Poetry Festival, May 16, 2015)

The Garden of Dreams
By Sonia Gutiérrez

In The Garden of Dreams,
when the heaviness
weighs pavement low,
only the winds can lift
these fingers
to touch the green
guava leaves.

The Earth's skin
calls these dormant
green hands to uproot crabgrass,
to pluck dry leaves,
and to water earthen pots.
Because here, there is no place
for folk to mope around
with a screaming
emoji face. Oh no!

Fifty feet away,
Ms. Rake, leaning against
the wall, hollers,
"These trees' branches
need shaking; let it rain
desert brown and yellow
all around you! Rake!"
And she's right!
Because if bodies dawdle
around aimlessly
in The Garden of Dreams,
weed vines will overtake
the dancing dwarf orange tree
and the guava trees'
white blossoms.
And the cawing crows
will most certainly
peck and eat
this year's purple
and green delights,
hanging

from the large-leaved fig trees.

In the dream garden,
birds are singing
from a far,
where Mrs. Ruby Red
Geranium's
dry petals peer through
the fleshy purple rose succulents;
her chapped lips
await the blue watering pot's
heavy drizzle that will make her roots
dance with delight.

But before these hands
tend the dream garden,
I reach for Tata Sun
who keeps us warm
and Nana Moon
who grows light
in her womb.
There is a brightness
in all the flowers
where I am intertwined;
this I know for certain
when my eyes meet Mr. Fern
in need of a trim.
And before I can get
my hands through his fronds,
I make sure I smother myself with rosemary
and am reminded everything will be just fine
because The Garden of Dreams
did not begin with me;
its seeds were passed
down to me,
keeper of the Earth.

El molcajete de mi abuela
By Ralph Haskins Elizondo

What once was a proud, sculptured Mexican mortar,
strong, and chiseled to last a thousand years,
is now a small humbled grey-pit shadow
holding a tiny pebble of a pestle on its concaved lap
ground down to a rounded rock.
Eons of ornery stone, born to grind
into submission decades of unrepentant
peppers in my grandmother's long kitchen,
she milled her seasons of salsas there,
since beyond the revolution; every chile-tomato taste,
an explosion of Villa's armies taking the field.
My grandfather's cavalry, charges again
to quell the uprising taking place
on the battlefield of my tongue.
The pits and pores hang on to all
the memories of flavors ever pressed.
I can still taste my childhood, and my mother's childhood,
both intertwined in cilantro,
but like my grandmother, time grinding away
at her skin, her organs, even stone wears out.
Ya puedes descansar amigo mío.

Ars Poetica
By Aurelia Lorca

The Heliopolis held 3,000 more passengers than capacity. She was the first ship to leave for Hawaii from Andalusia. How did they fit that many people? What models did they use? Bodies upon bodies. Like a slave ship. Except it was a slave ship. "Fine human freight," the newspapers called them to break the Asian work force. My grandfather's parents and his oldest brother, Juan, who was five years old, were escaping a kind of unfathomable poverty and oppression my father says I will never know, much less understand. There had been a famine and the Spanish government allowed such taking of Andaluzes- half savage *ordinarios y analfabetos* with too much Moorish blood. The ship returned to port because there was not enough food other than bread and coffee brewed with salt water, and the bones of arms, and the swollen bulges of bellies, crying with the pulse of filth and vomit and ocean. If I am quiet enough, I can smell the smells too and it will make me angry instead of grateful. Mothers wrapping their children tight in blankets, and fear. Stories of sick babies thrown overboard. The warmth of Hawaii was heat and anger: there was no land, it was a trick. Indentured servitude, a nicer way of saying slavery. The pain in their stomachs never went away. They gambled onto another ship for California, the state with a made-up name, and were given a choice: Hawaii or deportation back to Spain. They learned not to cry. They learned how to make the rest of their children become American.

*   *   *

There is no other way to say this.
What about words?
Words dreamt of and believed so strongly
that by the time they reach generations,
they believe they are true.
Unfamiliar morphemes, strange sounds do not translate.

My grandfather and his sisters and brothers would learn English.
Learn how to read and write a few words.
They would learn anything, have American first names,
though it would take them almost forty years to have the papers
to prove they were American born.
"Don't talk about the past," they all would say.
It all was better than feudalism and Spain.
It all was better than Franco and Spain.
"Don't talk about the past,"

though in 2014, the words
"Communist"
"Agitator"
"Bootlegger" are meaningless,
no longer subversive.
I want to scream.
I want to get drunk.

*   *   *

I want to scream for the dead,
all those who are lost to the history of the past
and the present. Like my father,
I am named after my father,
instead of my mother's father,
just so I do not carry the curse
of my great-uncle's name.

Juan Henares. I will say his name in Spanish.
I am not afraid. My grandfather and the rest of his siblings
all had American names.
They called him "John"—but only they were American.
He was illegal, as if any human being can be illegal.
I can see him now, 112 years old but not bent.
A giant, holding a cane
more like a weapon than anything else,
the way 'buelita, his mother, wore her rings.
I can hear his laughs at our American-ness,
how we sacrificed memory for the American Dream.
Yet, our *duende* is always with us.
No matter how hard we aspire to achieve bigger,
faster, more, and no matter how hard we try to forget.
He is all we do not speak of other than in the language of shame,
the language of silence. It has burned my tongue
with hives, and bitter red dots. Hence, I must speak,
I must give the words life. Nothing can soothe me
other than the violence of my words.
The struggle with language,
the struggle to find meaning. But where, where,
where should I begin? With my great-uncle Juan Henares?

Hence, here is the story: Juan Henares is a ghost who is 112 years old. He came from Lucena, a pueblo the size of a pea, outside of Cordoba. He came on the Heliopolis, the first ship to Hawaii that had to go back to port in Malaga because it was so poorly equipped. Though its maximum occupancy was supposed to be 1000 passengers, it carried him with another 3,891 Andalusians- peasants who the Spanish state characterized in newspapers as "shiftless dreamers" due to their Moorish blood. The ship went back to port because the people were only fed bread and coffee brewed with sea water- there was not enough food. How did they fit three thousand extra people on that ship? I cannot wrap my mind around it. The Honolulu newspapers called them "Human Freight" - "white" labor from the South of Spain, to break up the Asian workforce. They were going to make them Americans, white Americans, good Americans. But in Hawaii, there were whips and the workers were still starving. They never planned on staying. Some day they would return to Spain, when there was enough money. But Franco, he changed that. I am an accident of history.

*   *   *

Twenty years later, when Juan Henares
gave himself to the Sacramento river,
I wonder if his hat was still tilted,
drowning in the American Dream.
I have given him many names:
Juan Granada, Johnny Pride, The Gitano Stagger Lee.
He lives in all of us.
His name was Juan. He was neither a conquistador or a friar.
He was a Spaniard, an Andalusian, an invisible immigrant
whose history has been lost except for one photograph,
and a name that has been forgotten
as a way to remember.
As I search through my heart
to understand him, I hear his suicide cries.
I can hear him laughing because he is still here.
His story has been repeated over and over again.
Whenever we have been lost,
whenever we have failed,
whenever we have won.
In the curse of his name.

*   *   *

MAKE THEM AMERICANS,
MAKE THEM AMERICANS,
MAKE THEM AMERICANS,
MAKE THEM AMERICANS.
And that they did.
And that they did.
The made my grandfather
one of the first Hispanic general contractors on the Monterey Peninsula.
They made my father a community activist and affirmative action officer.
They made my father's twin, my uncle, a teacher in the prisons,
working with the students society did not want.
They made me, an American poet who is free to say,
remember, remember, remember.

Luna de Papel
By Leticia Hernandez-Linares

Ya salió la luna, ya salió la luna
luz en mi cara, mi alma desnuda
Hay vienen los poetas y las cantantes
vas a tener que contarles las penas

I tried to wrestle with the moon
y me mordió la lengua.

She pounded my poems into shards,
severing them. La luna se me metió
en la boca, pulling my tongue
for not being honest enough.

So I took up drawing, cut clothes out
for a paper doll. Teasing stories into
her pelo. La Poetisa, I call her,
loose strands tucked under pulp headwrap,
behind a griot mask. I painted it for her
to safely scavenge for aging books and hidden liner notes.

Ink on foot and finger y la calle her keyboard.
¡La vecindad! The neighborhood––la mera canción
that doesn't let the heart break. The refrain,
saludos to los revolucionarios, berets
teetering on their heads, sipping
nostalgia from ceramic mugs.

Los hermanos poetas yell metaphor,
stuff their angst into sermon. Las mujeres
craft medicine from liberated vocal chords.
La Poetisa strips the thorns from each
papier-mâché flower of a poem.

En la Misión, El Poeta Laureado embraces
the escritores he calls together to tie cantos
along la veinticuatro. Mission murals
diagram arteries and chi points. La Poetisa,
hides behind curtains of fog, watches

for Texidor to push his cane into the stars
turning on the sky so GGP can see when he shouts
out his window ¡abran los ojos cabrones! Lorna packs up
the waves, wheat pasting lines on the telephone poll.
Avotjca gets the call to bring the salve of her drum.

La Poetisa doles out frozen truths for you to lick
on a cold day. La memoria vuela
con las cuerdas del charango. I ask la luna
if I am made of paper, can I erase
the extranjeros building so high into the sky,
they block the stars on la veinticuatro.

hay vienen los poetas
y las cantantes
vas a tener que contarles las penas

La Poetisa distributes messages tied to her feet
landing at Galería to declarar
new poems under the full moon.
Everyone waiting. Filling the room
with our children now, small hands
keeping time, counting the years
when it was the poetry
that brought us together.

Ya salió la luna
ya salió la luna
luz en mi cara
mi alma desnuda
Hay vienen los poetas
y las cantantes
vas a tener que contarles las penas.

Ojo de Dios*
By Leticia Hernandez-Linares

-after Ana Teresa Fernández's *Hipsteria*
-para la Misión

1.

Sikuli. Dig for water, spin for sight.

Between nimble fingers, two sticks tied with yarn
hold Huichol spider web prayer. In the Mission––

it's become a trinket. Disoriented words, breathless
and incendiary clamor at 24th and Mission. We cover

the corners with confession. We have
succumbed to epidemic––es la Hipsteria.

That inablity to recognize our surroundings. Strangers
blocking the people's podium, where la gente

shoot voice into the air, in front of iron bars
holding down rebel bricks. Public transport serpent slithers
down the main drag during countless marches. Fists raised

at this convergence of crowd, megaphone, dance circle,
meeting place, some see Bart stop––we are at church.

Pero la Hipsteria. This malaise has struck before.
Almost saving us––converted souls calling their gods

by proper Aztec names snapping consonants, scripture
painted on their skin, moving meditation at the center

of commute and communion. Amidst cacophonous calls
for salvation, justice, a drink, pedimos, en el caos,

que no nos agarre la Hipsteria. But it persists,
paints us a new face.

2.

Sikuli. Dig for water, spin for sight.

Little girl squeezes Elmer's out of orange,
ties yarn into un ojo de dios.

I hum under my breath a childhood song
about questions. Un día yo pregunté, asked
my father where God is.

Holding up popsicle sticks to the light, a cross pulling
four directions together purports to offer
a window. Loose string. An unraveling.

Our church defiled. In the name of development,
owners don't solicit participation. Dice and privilege

pave the way to yes we will take it, at any price, slip in
between folding up store fronts, families walking
away––puro recuerdo packed up in boxes.

Spokes under newcomer feet bring spectacle.
Día de los muertos paints faces more like payasos now.

We move our feet furiously por la fe.
Our bounty drawn down from danza, onlookers
applauding––but it isn't a show.

3.

Sikuli. Dig for water, spin for sight.

Always block to block here, our son kicks the ball
a prism away from where boys finished a man

for being too broken. Little legs running
in unison––the chance to be a star. The goal

to score the ball, or settle one. Either way,

la Rose weaves ojos de dios out of paper,
focusing our attention on the bendiciones.

She hums songs about covered currents,
a buried cove that once curved

its waters in the form of a half moon. Mission Creek
ran until men covered it with dirt
to make way for dehydrated tangibles.

4.

Sikuli. Dig for water, spin for sight.

We swallow penas, talk to the veil
passing over the moon. Our throats brace

for distilled stinging, las comadres and I brindamos
the eclipse and our mothers as a man who waited hope
on the corner all day passes a woman who served disdain

at the coffee counter all day. Qué dios nos guarde
de la Hipsteria. Sikuli. Spinning words for sight.

Untying knots that make painted water fall
from the walls to shield us from contagion,
keeping the dirt out of our mouths.

*Ojo de dios, or God's eye, is a weaving made across two or more sticks and is
thought to have originated with the Huichol Indians of Jalisco, Mexico. The Huichol
call their God's eyes, Sikuli, which means "the power to see and understand things
unknown."

Ode to Portola
By Suzanna Huerta

Dusk calls me to walk San Bruno Avenue
just as the distant fog rolls in pastel hues, mutes
the horizon. The neighborhood slows, space
opens on the sidewalk, a letting go from the day,
collective sigh of the end. Palega baseball diamond
fills with middle-school teams,
and market owners bring in the produce. Collectors
scavenge the pallets, cardboard boxes
stained with ripe fruit juice and pastry
grease. Kids make the most of before dark,
barrel downhill on Silver, skateboards
scrape pavement when they turn on a dime
before traffic. Everywhere there is a twin energy
of longing to rest, and of desire to capture what's left
of a dying day. A final sweep of the gutter, taking out
the garbage before night falls. Old women and dutiful daughters
walk side by side, uphill, against wind and wrapped
in parkas. Yapping toy dogs lead on nearly invisible leashes,
as owners trail behind with compostable plastic bags. Nail shops
draw their gates, liquor store corners ignite with neon and beer
logos. Buses unload the cargo of day shifters, most staring
at their feet as they make their way home, make their way
into automatic, guided by hunger, exhaustion or need to
connect or disconnect somewhere inside. Many will disappear
tonight in front of screens or inside bottles or smoke. Some will
do homework late into another breaking morning
of hustle and grit. I spot an ashen pigeon settling itself into
a puddled pothole warmed by asphalt and a fading patch of sun.
He dips and shimmies in the stale, muddied water, oil slick
wings budding droplets dirtied with exhaust fumes and filth,
stretches out each wing like an elegant dove, extends both
legs, first the left, then the right, a glorious stump, before
flying off and over the deli rooftop.

El Norte
By Paul Lobo Portugés

For the children of El Salvador, Guatemala, and Honduras.

When he was 8 in the white heat of El Infiernito
guarding their fruit truck they murdered his father
and the squawking blue birds of his young hope
flew away into the gut of lovely night
and the proud red plums he held rolled down
the blood alley as rain fell like broken feathers

When he was in the flesh of his blue youth
songs turned to skeletons in his best friend's eyes
they smiled as they slit her white naked throat
and stuffed panties in her red mouth of dreams
that dia de los muertos she became the flowers of graves.
seeing a body was nothing anymore

When he was 12 narcos beat him blind
so he couldn't see their skulls of red death
his tearless baby cousins could only look on
Santa Muerte made him lick the white thighs of crack
"You'll feel freed like a bird entering
 a red cloud in the bruise of blue night"

His dirty government can't pull up its pants.
"If your house is burning, jump out the window"
so he took the lazy train of hopeful skeletons
with a handful of plums and his invisible hope
and crossed the red white and blue border of eagles
like a beautiful feather on the veins of lonely wind.

Mission Creek
By Cesar Love

A stream that crossed half the City
From the slope of Twin Peaks to the marsh of Mission Bay
Today it's forgotten from all but the oldest maps

The water choked by storm drains and sewers
Its gurgle silenced beneath asphalt and trucks
Strangled below the overpass echo

On days of long rain, a memory splashes
Blue herons and egrets, flickering minnows
Ohlone canoes returned from the Bay

On Division Street, campers and old cars park overnight
Shopping carts and urban tents crouch on hard cement
People of the margin sleep here

The lost creek talks to a boy, one who skips stones
The creek tells him, find a flat rock and throw it.
Hurl it to bring back the herons, trout, and dragonflies

Golden Cages
By MamaCoAtl (Silvia Parra)

If life is a dream
I must still be sitting
By the edge of my bed
Looking out the window
Down on Folsom Street
Thinking

The day looks just fine from here
It even seems unusually clear
There are no people on the street It's midmorning
And everybody is busy chasing a dream
Struggling to pay the rent
Stressing to find the secrets of success or
Satisfied with having a thousand face book friends

Denying that we are so alone
Severed from the very source of life
We are too alone
And we are drowning in our plastic bags
We poison the air that we breathe
We move feces with the water that we'll drink
We criminalize the hand that feeds us and
We find it fun to kill

From here we watch the world falling apart all around us
From behind the comfort of our coffee cups
And we hail de revolutions that we long to be a part of
But we don't dare leave the couch
Our pretty leash, our doggy treats
Our fantasies and our addictions if you please
Our consuming habits and our ancestral guilt

And we are so alone in our electronic pages
Portraying the ideal image of ourselves
We are too alone behind our educated trenches
Defending and preserving philosophies that have already failed;
Like the economy of extraction,
Worldwide degradation and mass distraction

Bowing to the patriot and his deadly masquerade.

But

Even though there is blood in our hands,
Even though all this horror in our name
Oh how I long to forgive myself!
And be humble enough to ask the forgiveness
Of all those people whose skin is the color of the Earth.
Forgive us for this terrible legacy
This Manifest Destiny
Forgive us
Pachamama, Great Tonanzin,
Forgive us
We long to forgive ourselves
Right now.

Lamento del Wirikuta
Por MamaCoAtl (Silvia Parra)

Por el cerro del quemado
Vimos florecer al sol
Con el pecho renovado
Sus verdores germino,

Por el cerro del Quemado
Es que vinimos a cantar
Para que tenga buen camino
En su paso cenital.

Por el cerro del Quemado
Enardecido mi Corazón!
First Majestic Corporation
Minera transnacional
Quiere triturar los huesos
De mi Madre viva
Mi tierra natal

La platera Canadiense
Tiene justificación
Es su bolsa de valores
Su mandato de nación
No les importan las flores
Pues ganan dinero
De la destrucción.

Marakate Kawitero
Abuelo en el sueno del existir
Guardiancito de la ciencia
Pariente del Río y del Maíz
Kayumari Venadito
Hermano nuestro
Sabio Mayor
Curandero Hikurito
Lava nuestra cara
Con tu resplandor.

El balance en esta vida

Se mantiene con amor
Con la gracia compartida
Con la bendición del sol
Curando nuestras heridas
Caminando con honor
Por el cerro del Quemado
Agradecido mi corazón.

Oración
Por Rafael Manriquez

Esto de no llegar a ninguna parte
me produce vértigos
esto de ser soslayado
por el de arriba me deprime

Mi Diosa Dios
Dame la inspiración
Para mantenerme firme

Hazme humilde
Y honradamente feliz
Con lo que vivo y logro

Es tanto ver y obrar
Con todos los sentidos
Es tan grandioso saber
Agradecerlo, apreciarlo
Compartirlo
Y es tan poco inteligente
Sentirse vencido

Mi Diosa Dios
Dame la capacidad
De ser sencillo
Y no anhelar grandezas
Dame salud, claridad
Inteligencia, valor
Te pido

Mi Diosa Dios todo esto
Esta adentro de mí
Y de cada uno
Y el privilegio de la música
Y la poesía es tan grande

Dame pues la capacidad
De apreciarlas, sin esperas
Ni sueños de grande

Solo quiero seguir por la vida
Encontrándolas
Solo quiero seguir mi bendita voz
Mi música y mi poesía
Compartiéndolas sin ambicione.

Translation of Gracía Lorca's Drawing of a Weeping Moon
By Arturo Mantecón

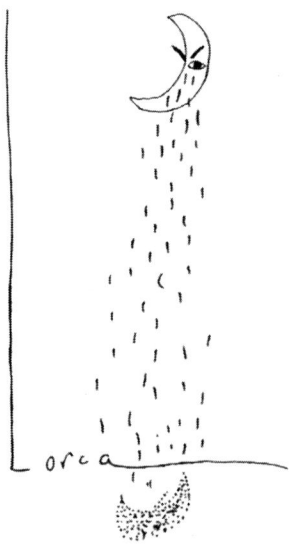

The waning moon,
cut and wounded
by the light-thieving
earth,
llorando e
implorando
to be made
whole...
weeps
from its one
black-browed,
sun-discovered eye.

Its tidal tears
¡negras como sangre!
caen sobre la tierra,
to spatter there
the shape
of a dark
crescent pool.

Translation of García Lorca's Drawing "Agua Sexual"
by Arturo Mantecón

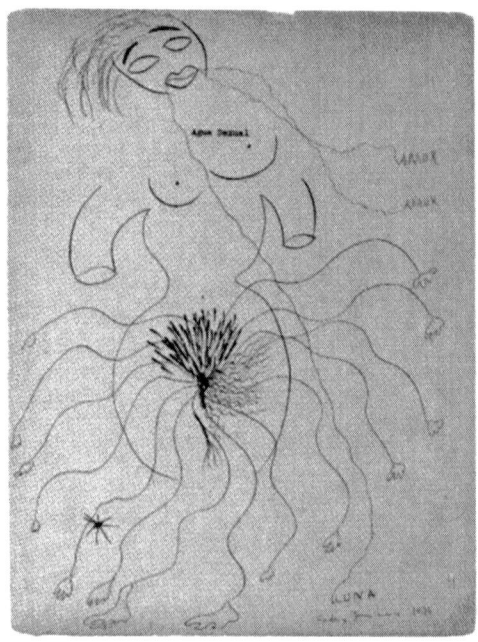

The water! The waters!
The jets and eruptions
from the maidenhead,
fountainhead
of sex...
black streaming
woman sperm,
avid leeches of desire
or sleek rapid
flying eyebrows,
root and cilia,
water blood
of vaginal tides,
fragmented
uterine tissue,
mucin, potassium
and oceanic salts.
Behold the bacteria of love,
the vaginal flora
that she extends like petal hands
at the ends of sinuous vines,
four-fingered blossom hands
bursting from her
center of the universe
vulva,
twelve hands of the lunar year.

And two are her feet
of lobed leaves,
the fourteen extremities
of the forgetfulness of the moon…
fourteen days waxing,
fourteen day waning.
The water! The waters!
The spurts and ejaculations,
the fluid seed of the lion's teeth
casting scented money, fertile coins
to all the willful winds.
And no one can avert
his eyes
from this amputated, sparse-haired,
tail of a horse, unkempt hag
of a slut siren,
the bountiful beauty
of vast vacant eyes,
her imbalanced breasts
full of the

LOVE AND THE BLOOD OF THE MOON
that proceeds from tight lips,
in tethered words spoken
unspoken falling to the ground,
trailing the strings of gravity
AMOR, AMOR, LUNA, LUNA.

At Dusk
By Norm Mattox

the murmurings of the neighborhood…
listening to 'una bulla',
a cacophony of sounds,
music, conversation,
silverware against empty plates,
the sound of content, full bellies...
the same chattering sparrows
recounting their day
like no one is listening,
only chirping,
barking like dogs
at the setting sun.
what languages
are we speaking?
dog?
bird?
tree?
human?
breeze?
motor?
en inglés?
all in spanish?
no matter!
the earth knows only
that it's time for the stars
to have their say.

Tres Niñas: Diaries
By Mariana McDonald

An estimated 600,000 children, 150,000 in the last year alone, have been separated from one or both parents by the current U.S. detain-and-deport policies. Human Impact Partners (HIP), 2013.

Yasmin G.

Mami didn't come back home last night.
Tia says she's gone away. In the dark
I heard the word *detention.* I can
hear the sad in Papi's voice.
You must help me now, he says. Because
you're ten years old. A big girl.

In the dark I don't feel big. I cry
for Mami, call to her. Papi's always tired
and sad, though he tries to be so happy.
Nena, he tells me, *you are my treasure*,
as he walks me to school in the morning dark.
He can't drive. Doesn't have a license.

Tonight we'll go to Dairy Queen for ice cream.
I'm going to make believe that Mami's there.

Patricia H.

Papi kissed me when he left
for work last week.

He still has not come
home. I'm all alone
till Mami's finished working,
helps me with my homework.

She said that Papi's gone
back home to where *Abuela*
birthed him, where

"the mountains feed the soul."

I don't think that's fair.
I want him here.

Ana Z.

Mom's in jail and now Dad's in detention.
Tia Luz is watching me, though she's alone
and always working. I'm thirteen and I don't

need a sitter. But this way I can stay out of
the system. I think I'm watching her as much
as she is watching me. I was born here,

I know how to manage. But
I don't like it,
not
   one
      bit!

I want
   to see
      my family!

A Weed in a Garden About to Get Plucked
By Lupe Méndez

Here, the cicadas called
in each direction,
louder than the wind
the crackle of footfall
smiling slighted conversations,
I am the Dandelion.

The sun, painted in yellow,
brought out ritual
children flying kites.
People blanketed meals,
soft grass grew around.
We are the Pennyworts.

Been here longer
than the neighbors have.
Watched as the languages
flipped summersaults,
once German. Once English.
We are the Burclovers.

Now Spanish. Now Tagalog.
- respect always spoken,
understood, pronounced.
Now crickets don't symphony.
Winds grow cold, even trees tremble.
I am the Chickweed.

See you running
these people out of time,
raising the rate
the way you plant fake
ideas, scatter seeds.
I am the Dallis grass.

Immature, rushed, weak
conversations, smile slightly.
No one else wants to stick
around the block.

Left around to bear witness,
I am a Purslane.

You're eroding what was here.
So, go ahead, try.
Take me from my home.
I used to bathe in the drops,
bask in the rays.
I am Goosegrass.

You want a new garden
in my property,
buy me out with poison water,
liquor me up by the roots,
pluck me from my abdomen.
I am Spurge.

You have to know
this has always been my home,
I'll be here, scarred if I must,
hidden in the underground,
I will always outgrow you.
I am an Ironweed.

Chicanos in a Museum
By Adela Najarro

And this time it was different.
Perla, Bilma, Clarissa, along with
Juvenal, two Alejandros, and un Ivan
walked into a palace of fine arts, a museum
of old depictions, depictions de la vida
y el coraje, paint on canvas, light reflected
pigments, an installation of a kitchen with posole
y los frijoles de tu mamá. They weren't seeking
job applications para trabajar toward
an American dream where they innocuously
wait to pick up paper towel trash
strewn across marble counters and floors,
and this time they weren't hidden
behind wallboard tinted hues
of indifference and invisibility.
They walked the halls; the halls
of a museum, el museo de Young, ese
museo de San Francisco. Respectability,
finance, approval of Chicano
art and its exhibit. Un special
que no estaba en K-Mart, pero allí
donde siempre estuvo: en el arte de la gente
los cuales fueron chavalitos
como estos camindo those hallways right
then and there. These kids didn't stare
at European landscapes choked by
industrial era smog beautified sunsets.
They didn't have to wonder why
bucolic cows rollick on rolling hills.
They didn't marvel at the silkiness tone
of fair white skin and embroidered
tapestry lace. Today esos Chicano
chavalitos, esos bilingual,
bicultural, Chicano, Mejicano, Latino,
Latina, American kids saw themselves,
not white, not wannabe white, but themselves
pintados y representado by those who
had come before. La familia, la Raza,

los antepasados reaching forward
and through to La Bilma, La Perla through paintings
on a wall, an electric fire connection.
Today los artistas, Chicano artists,
had a show, an entire exhibit, grants,
artist-in-residency titles, a whole show.
Three rooms, a band, and two lectures
para esos Chicanos, esos allí de las calles,
saliendo de esas mismas calles para pintar
nuestro futuro, that future where we all stand
looking up at the hills as they burn
a flame reaching toward the sun.

My Mother's Voice is Banging in My Head
By Adela Najarro

Let el pasado be el pasado. Just go on.
Forward. Enjoy yourself. ¡Viva la vida!
And the sky is a startling robin egg's blue,
and I could go down to the beach,
a San Francisco always cool and windy,
just right for a walk beach. See sand crabs
bubble as the slide of a wave
returns to the deep blue sea. I could
be happy! Why write about disappointment
hitting like a punch in the stomach
or the inability to breath that sets in
after betrayal? It never stops.
We only switch places, venues,
and parts in the story. Today una migrante
working the fields, tomorrow
you're fired and can't pay the mortgage.
No matter—either it's happening right now
or later to someone else.
Injustice is the way of the world.
Glass storefronts twist our reflections
while skyscrapers block the sun.
And we are unfed and unkempt,
in a labyrinth of unknowing,
always seeking. I give to you
the robin's egg, the cloudless sky.
I give to you four steps outside
on a moderately warm August afternoon
when the cat next door asks for a scratch
on its back. But this will not stop
a tiny pebble from finding its way
into your shoe.

Amor is More Than a Kiss
By Joe Navarro

When you are with me
I am at my best
When I feel pain
Your presence soothes me
When my heart is hollow
You fill it with your breath
When all feels lost
I find everything in your smile
When I am alone
Your voice accompanies me
When I look into your eyes
I remember our youth

When you feel pain or sadness
I feel it too
When you reach for the sky
I want to help lift you
When you experience joy
I am happy
When we see the world together
We share the promise of a just world
When we kiss
Love feels complete
A veces me siento como
Amor es todo y
Todo es amor
Yet I realize that
Amor is more
Than a kiss.

Eviction in San Francisco an Ekphrastic Poem
By Gerardo Pacheco Matus

a broken mirror is left
amongst a pile of garbage.

my mother's treasure is now,
a useless heap of memories.

bits and pieces of time shuttered
left on the peed pavement
of the city of San Francisco.

a reminder of a whole life
left on the street corner
for pedestrians' to scavenge.

"50 years of living here
in this city is a whole life,"
my old mother says,

as she and I struggle
to rearrange
boxes of photographs and birth
certificates
into her little Toyota
that has no more room
for our memories.

her tiny frame splits into a hundred
images scattered on the floor.

I can see my mother's smile
a hundred times
as she tightens her jaws
whenever she says, "it's time…
to move on with our lives."

what's a mother's treasure,
but her children and her home?

I Claim The Desert
By Gerardo Pacheco Matus

i claim the desert as my home.
i claim this cacti world as mine.

the old bones turning to dust
under the old saguaro tree belong to me.

the wooden crosses without names
are part of my kingdom.

every single shallow grave belongs to me.
every single forgotten corpse is mine.

i claim all of the dead undocumented
women, men and children left behind
as part of my kingdom.

i claim all of the dry bones
and all of the pain that lives
between mandibles and clavicles.

i claim the metal wall as mine---

i claim these rape trees
that bloom behind the metal wall
as part of my endless kingdom.

i claim all of the pain,
all of the tears,
all of the prayers.

i claim la mujer vieja,
who weeps in the arroyo as mine,

i claim all of the unknown,
the sick, the old, the young
the crippled, the innocent.

i claim the dry water holes,
the dry, empty fields
and the dead cows as mine.

i claim dead as my queen
and thirst as my punishment.
i claim this desert as mine.

Age Old Poetry
By Melinda Palacio

We all write one.
Nancy wrote hers at 25. Her adult face and
costume settling in, long hair and harem pants,
a staple to carry her into her rocking chair days.

I write my poem twenty years later.

In photographs, I notice bald patches of pulled-out,
death-white hair. My thinning locks looks like an odd border,
a map to an island, pushed out of existence, where silences and
quiet moments make me see the world as if for the first time.

A quiet moment and the words of a young girl, 25, come back to haunt me
like an echo of a dream deferred.

    You're just like my mom, she says.
I look into her Dominican eyes and wonder at the virginity I wanted to shed
by a Dominican boy who respected me too much at age seventeen.

The Caribbean girl with swaying palm-tree curls
does not worry about face creams
or tweezing random strands of gray.
She merely laughs when I tell her she is my daughter.

[Untitled]
Silverio Pelayo

1.
Blessed Are We
Nestled in-between
The sky and the earth
God's hands
Clasped together
In prayer

2.
Have you seen the way
Birds fly
How they navigate
This reality
Every graceful movement
Is a brush stroke
Held by the steady hand
Of your eye
Every flutter
A dab of magic
Unfurling
The bud
Of possibility's
Becoming
Every flap of the wing
A blessing
To those
Below

3.
Your story is a snake
That sheds
The death
Of deception
It is a lightning bolt
Fashioned from the golden fibers
That thread
The infinite sky

Of your heart
It is a fire
Carried on the wings
Of hawks vision
Set ablaze
The dawning
Of a new day.

At Home (para Dieguito)
By René Peña-Govea

You were born at home on a cinder block and plywood bed
on a hill that smelled so much of coffee it steeped your dreams,
but you still wonder tremulously if that aroma-memory can be true.
And some pictures of it, your city,
flash like furious moths,
like afterimages against your eyelids
and you need another person to remember with you,
to say, I too was there when
those men the color of raw sugar
gripped their toes
across the metal bar of the tall tall TALL swing-set in Dolores Park,
their bird-thin shadows
dancing liquid above the sand
and the congueros played on,
implacable under the pendulous date palms,
and the beautiful golden boys on their velvet beds of grass
devoured the sky
in those epidemic years.
That disease only called at your doorstep
when they told you, heavy faced,
that your preschool teacher had died,
and they did say AIDS,
softly though,
like snow.
And when Hugh Masakela sang "Bring Back Nelson Mandela" on the radio
on your way to spoon miso and tahini
out of cylinders at Rainbow
it was daytime,
the popcorn clouds seeded with gold,
because your dad only worked nights as needed
but your parents could still raise their child in the belly,
or more like the southern toenail,
of this glittering dragon-city by the Bay.
Down by the ballpark,
before it existed,
you skipped past trailers to get to Tick Tock
where they handed you a glazed donut
and a cheese and pickle sandwich on waxed paper
which you ate at a scarred desk in a tiny cabin under the Third Street Bridge with

your dad,
the bridge-tender.
Sometimes, you did sleep there,
on a wooden bed fastened to the wall, Army blanket burritoed around you,
the slap slap of the water on the pilings thrumming dark and luxuriously,
my city, my city, my city.
In this city, snail-trails remain,
invisible mostly but lustrous as glycerin to the rememberers:
The library where your sister made her debut at age five on a four-stringed guitar
your mom taught her and you on the accordion
still stands,
but it's re-sculpted, re-occupied, re-envisioned,
 and they whitewashed Victor Jara's face and other gente right off the wall
and erased the newspaper photo of girl-you marching outside the building, which
in leaner times had to be defended by children with signs.
So many photos were never taken,
so many people sluiced away
and the choices seem to lie there, bright as gleaming olives:
Rage against gentrification on furious websites, carnal protests, or elusive ballots;
walk down 24th street simmering with bile as you shell out a dollar or more for a
concha and steel yourself because you are a native, carajo!
But what of those images that rise like sharp ash,
like scream-bright flowers on oilcloth
in the middle of the day?
Maybe you can never go home again,
but what if you stayed, and your home up and left you?
Your baby was born at home in this narrow city,
like your sister before him and you before her
and so your choice is clear and you must bear it and
Claim it, your city.
Not without silvery ribbons of sadness
or full-throated pain
or the occasional
fucktheellisact dancing hotly on your tongue,
but for your son,
also,
with a trumpet on Carnaval morning,
ink in El Tecolote,
words sweet as elote
as you tell him
about home.

Dr. Jesus' Presents: The Chupacabra Learns His ABC(Ch)'s
By Juan Manuel Perez

A is for *Aztlan*
>   across the border, way beyond
B is for brown
>   'cause chupacabras stick around
C is for *canciones*
>   like the ones I sing for you
CH is for *cholos*
>   always tat their skin in blue
D is for *diablo*
>   like the name they yell at me
E is for *enchiladas*
>   a plate of those, then you'll see
F is for *fiestas*
>   like the ones I get to go
G is for *gritos*
>   like the ones I like to throw
H is for *hijos*
>   like those left in Mejico
I is for immigration
>   or the ignorant who just don't know
J is for *jalapeños*
>   great with beans, it's understood
K is for killers
>   like those vatos in the hood
L is for *locos*
>   'cause they want to take me down
LL is for *la llorona*
>   so watch out or you'll be drowned
M is for *menudo*
>   yes, I think I'd like a bowl
N is for *nueces*
>   crack them open, check for mold
Ñ is for *niños*
>   scream at them until your blue
O is for *ojitos*
>   like the pretty ones on you
P is for *piñatas*
>   filled with candies, kids all know

Q is for *quesadillas*
      one too many and you'll blow
R is for reckless
      that's what mami says I am
RR is for *perro*
      like the dog eating from cans
S is for *sanchas*
      of which I have so much
T is for *trucha*
      for so-and-so and such-and-such
U is for ugly
      like the "me" they think they see
V is for *vatos*
      like the ones shooting at me
W is for *wacha*
      'cause that's all that they can do
X is for x-rays
      gonna break some bones or sue
Y is for *Yaya*
      code for "Laura" in the hood
Z is for *zacate*
      mowing lawns, my livelihood

So now I know my alphabet
Makes me cool with no regret
So little *cholos* stay in school
Be a reader, not a fool.

La Morenita
By reina alejandra prado

La Morenita was bound to become a revolutionary icon
Had to figure out how to exist in a colonial imaginary
Literally shed her snake skin to become muxer
Diosa embodied as an Indígena
A woman, the church could embrace
I know,this sounds blasphemous to some
Ni modo, it's in my DNA to challenge patriarchy

Maybe I can learn something from La Morenita
Unleash the power de Tonantzin
To burn down empires
Like she did in 1810, 1910, 1966, 1994, …
From the ashes, we emerge

Learn from her to honor mi piel morena
Keep what's true in my corazón
Chalé with the secrecy
How about you accept my duality
that I speak with *a forked tongue*
como decíaAnzaldúa
otra morenita querida.

Of Dogs and Mexicans
By Joseph Rios

Part One:

While driving by Bulldog Lane, you remember Enrique.
He lived on a second floor apartment overlooking Barstow Ave.
Every morning, your father would roll up in truck towing trailer
and beat on the horn until Enrique slid open his window,
threw out a plastic bag with his lunch, crawled half out
and leaped to the ground below. Once up, he'd jump
a six foot fence to get to the truck. Every morning he did this.
But when your father dropped him off at the end of the day,
he'd always leave Enrique at the front door. Neither explained why.

Just then, you remember the day Enrique took a shit
in what was left of the foil he used to wrap his burrito.
He did it in the backyard where the willow tree hung
over the fence and onto the golf course behind each house.
He folded the aluminum neatly and brought the package
to the front and deposited it in the green garbage can.
You and your older brother had a good laugh about it in English.
Enrique just nodded and looked out the window rubbing his forearm
covered in dust and fading, black-lined, nearly illegible tattoos.

Part Two:

The more important part of the story, you will remember,
occurred the following week when you and your brother went back
to the house. You found the old white lady in some sort of pajama
ensemble, toting a hose pistol with the garbage can on its side.
She looked up at you, her hair already sticking to her face,
breathing heavily through her mouth to communicate her frustration.
As your father's son, and in your best English, you greet her
and ask her what happened. She tells you someone put dog poop
in a foil bag and then put it in her garbage can. After a week
of one hundred degree days, the foil bag burst open and sprayed
the inner walls. You don't know how, but that's not important.

The dark matter baked and fumed in the heat for those seven days.
So there she was, still in her night clothes just before noon, greeting
her gardener's son in slippers stained with Enrique's week old shit.
You're older now. Almost two decades have gone by since that morning
and you can think of no other moment that offered you such satisfaction.

In those days, Enrique moved ten dollar sacks of cheap weed.
He did time. Your father knew. He had done the same.
Everyone's hands were dirty, you say, recognizing the poetic appeal.
One morning, you don't pick up Enrique. You ask your father why
and he tells you the police got him. They chased him near Bulldog Lane.
He barricaded himself in that same apartment he jumped from so many times.
When Enrique refused to come out, the police sent their dog after him.
The dog entered the room where Enrique waited, armed with a kitchen knife.
The animal charged him and he thrust the knife into it's side. The dog eventually
died. You didn't see Enrique ever again. Thinking now, you recall a story your
grandfather told you about restaurants with signs out front that read, "No dogs
or Mexicans allowed." You can't understand why this story comes to mind.
They're not even related, you think to yourself, not at all.

Oda a la tortilla
Por Jorge Salas

gran regalo

de la Diosa

Xilonen

de maíz

amarillo

blanco

morado

rojo

de todos

colores

tamaños

sabores

tortillitas

redonditas

calientitas

o en tostadas

tacos

flautas

memelitas

chalupitas

eres plato

cubiertos

servilleta

eres todo

en uno

y uno

para todos.

When Miguelito Should Have Been Sleeping
By Yaccaira Salvatierra

and his *tías de México* and his mother gathered around
the kitchen table, stories drifting toward his room
like *cafecito* vapor, he leaned against his door to listen.
When he first heard about how his orphaned grandmother

was her own godmother's *criada*, how she would fall asleep
while scrubbing *los pinche pisos*—knees and knuckles
tired and raw from scratching against the cracked
clay floor—he imagined himself standing

next to his grandmother's child-body: limp limbs, ragged-
heavy like a drenched mop's clothed tentacles;
he imagined himself ordering the opening of the earth,
¡Ábrete! ¡Ábrete, trágatela ahora cuando está dormida!

When he heard how his grandfather would shove a kicking
and screaming laughter into a plastic bag on those days
he left to work on foreign lands, leave his daughters
without half a giggle because Miguelito's grandfather

would need laughter more, he imagined himself
waiting for his grandfather's hurried stride. He imagined
flinging himself toward the thick plastic—tearing it open
with a fork—letting laughter bounce back into the bellies

of children because what are children without laughter?
When he learned how Fausto, the catechist, would lure children
into praying un *"Padre nuestro"* while their fathers were leaving
one by one, he wondered why his *tías* would say, *Dios lo bendiga.*

But when he first heard about his mother clubbing
the neighbor's stray pig to death when she was a child,
he wept, but not for the pig.

Aves Errantes
Por Betty Sánchez

¿De dónde vengo? ¿A dónde voy?
No tiene importancia mi destino
No pienso más allá de éste momento
El sonido del hambre en las entrañas
Me impide vislumbrar un posible futuro
Deambulo en las aceras
Mendingando un pedazo de pan
Vendo mi dignidad por unos pesos
Mi aspecto lastimero te molesta
Si intento acercarme desvías tu mirada
Tu indiferencia no me vuelve invisible
Seguiré siendo figura cotidiana
En el paisaje urbano
Víctima del abandono y del maltrato
De la explotación y del desprecio
Mi presencia incomoda
Expone a una sociedad farisaica
Plagada de desdén e intolerancia
Que ha fracasado en proteger
A los débiles y desamparados
Es más fácil ignorarme
Hacer una mueca de fastidio
Para reducirme a un silencio
Que la oscuridad se llevara consigo
Las parejas que buscan los rincones
Se alejan presurosas
Al descubrir mi cuerpo agazapado
Envuelto en atuendo andrajoso
Y sombras desgastadas
Inhalo aerosoles nocivos
Para transformar mis monstruos
En hadas madrinas
Que me concederán volar
Y escapar de ésta realidad
Que llevo a cuestas
Que destiñe mis sueños
Que me aplasta y me impide
Sentir pensar vivir

Soy una planta silvestre
Que brota de las grietas del asfalto
Un ave errante que vaga sin rumbo
Una multitud sin identidad ni patria
Un fenómeno social que seguirá en aumento
Soy un niño de la calle.

Tres De Julio
Por Natalie Sánchez Valle

La llamaron loca por criar a sus hijos sin un padre
Le dijeron que no podía criar a sus hijos sola
Porque, ¿qué iba a decir la gente?
Juzgaron, criticaron

Hasta familiares le dejaron de llamar
No sabían si teníamos donde dormir o comida para comer

Pero aquí estamos 13 años después
Mi madre y mis dos hermanos, más fuertes que nunca

Por eso, no me asusta si me llaman loca por creer en mi misma
Si mi mamá pudo sola, sobresalir, luchar día con día, ¿yo por qué no?

No se necesita un padre para criar una familia.
Se necesita amor, ternura y atención.
Yo me surtí porque tuve lo triple.
Mi mamá y mis dos hermanos.

Guerrillero
Por John Santos

(para Alfonso Texidor)

El guerrillero nace recitando poesía
contemplando la belleza de lo que se llaman esta vida.
Saboreando la injusticia por primera vez,
grita en alta voz que no aceptamos la estupidez.
Se dedica fuertemente al movimiento del amor.
Viene abriendo caminos con el enfoque y su bastón.
Tumba al enemigo con su pluma y su visión
y vive siempre en el profundo del colectivo corazón.

No Soy Combatiente*
Por John Santos

(for Mercedes Sosa)

No soy guerrillero, pues las armas me asustan.
Al ver sangre el dolor me condena.
Pero del alma yo ofrezco todo mi ser
pa que reine la paz sobre la madre tierra.

Como el colibrí, de rama en rama, busco la dulzura de la vida.
Yo sigo la frescura del aire, mira que nadie intente alejarme de la enramada.
El campo veo con manos agradecidas.
Siento como si fuera mi altar,
donde susurro mis rezos más profundos
que el mundo sane a cada uno de sus heridas.

No soy guerrillero, ni soy un combatiente,
por eso digo que mi credo es la amistad.
Pero si pisan sin respeto a mi gente,
como una fiera defendería ¡la libertad!
¡Eh, ya basta de hacer daño a mi gente!
No soy ¡combatiente!

* *No Soy Combatiente* is a musical composition
composed by John Santos (2009)
published by Guataca Music, BMI
arranged by Pavel Urkiza
from the CD Filosofía Caribeña Vol.1
by The John Santos Sextet
Machete Records (2011)

Fading Sett
By Graciela Serna

I descended into
the heart of the city.
An enthused child
willingly consuming
the mores of the Mission.
Vibrant colors
nurtured,
cultivated,
and
paved my path
to be a painter
a peddler
a poet
Valencia, Folsom, Van Ness and Bartlett St.
all led to my door.
They were
the very veins
that integrated my life blood
and embellished my soul.
Allowing my phalanges
to sprout roots
into the canvasses and seams of the city,
garnishing galleries
with offerings
of pictures, patterns, and prints

From my womb
sprang my finest objets d'art.
Delivered into the embrace of the bay
Cradled by the arms of the barrio
Scrubbed by the soft morning rain
Entrusted to the transit deities
Their task,
to join the creative process
that WAS the Mission

For now my heart cries out,

like El Grito de Dolores!
A paramount pallette
splashed with dollar bill green
is smearing the storefronts and taquerias
Transforming el pueblo
into a central processing unit
Sequestering the rhythmic pulsation
of La Misión
Removing the lifeline
that ran through my veins,
and that of my children.
We are being expelled
removed from that
which was nurtured
cultivated,
and paved
long ago
The uprooting of the Mission
has begun
Gentrification 101
Where vibrancy once prevailed
dull colors envelop my scope
As I drift away
with notice in hand
I turn to take
One last glance at
my home
My heart
My Mission.

Tahui!
by Nina Serrano

For Francisco X. Alarcon

"Tahui!," calls Francisco X Alarcon
we respond with, "Tahui!"
carried on the echoing winds
in the four directions,
and above and below

Holy vibrations over the California
hills mountains canyons and deserts
creeks lakes, rivers and sea
Over fields of growing
lettuce brocolli celery and grapes
Over trees bearing
oranges pears plums
and swaying palms heavy with dates

Francisco's call
heard by young and old
Gathers us in the ether and ambiance
of floating ancient dusty remains
for poetry community creativity and justice
Speaking words that sing to Mother Earth
exploding stars
in the constantly expanding universe

Francisco is not waiting for laurel leaves
He labors for poetry constantly
If crowned his work will not change
He will continue as long as he breathes
to call, "Tahui!"
We will respond, "Tahui!"
in the four directions
and above and below.

Amigo Equis
By Stephanie Sherman

You wrap your tattoos around me
(those black and red *códices*),
and I purr, my painted lady,
en tu casa que huele a coco y copal
and sometimes we fuck but mostly
we gossip about your gay boys,
and bad art and my *artistas,*
until we decide
to dress up like *la Llorona y el Santo*
and head out on Shotwell
like a strange old couple
who no longer love each other that way
and never loved each other that way
but laugh at each other's jokes
without speaking.

Con tu máscara plateada y rosa en la boca,
you fasten my white wig
and powder my breasts
para verme mas güera que una calavera
mas gringa que el sonido de mi apellido.

Me dices chapis y te digo panzón,
como si yo fuese Kahlo y tú Rivera
and we buy Frida kitsch and *guayabas*
that perfume your kitchen.
We scour the thrift shops
in all of the Mission,
and you make eyes with the taco boy
as I order it *al pastor con una porción*
de aguacate.

Viejito querido, this is our rhythm:
My visits to your quickly disappearing apartment
(with its aging HIV latino queens
and their succulents)
that will soon dissolve into luxury condos.
Then, I will remember the perfume

of your pink sheets smelling of sex and lavender
where I have napped countless afternoons
on your chest
in the heart
of the Mission.

El problema
By John Oliver Simon

The problem is that information's money
each pair of eyes thrust at pathetic wafers
of smartphones — todos los commuters en BART —
pays for each tick of life a candle's flicker

so geeks get rich and Richie Rich gets richer
la Misión bendita con rayos de sol
is bang of gavel SOLD to the highest bidder
María, José y el niñito Chuy

squeezed into homelessness nos importa qué
the artists follow, bearded hipsters fleeing —
all I have to set against that is two girls
from Salvador and Todos Santos and East

Oakland and the Iron Triangle who caught
fire with poetry in second and fifth
grades and now have full rides to UCLA —
one here, one there to shine and lead the struggle.

Viva el Mole con Guajolote!
By Ricardo J. Tavarez

-To *Manuel Maples Arce*

Colorado   Almendrado
Emaciated ghosts of archbishops and viceroys
Drift on Pre-Columbian aromas
Rattling spoons on cobblestones
Dragging copper pots
Aching for Aztec gold
Pangs satiated by kitchen saints of colonial Puebla

Amarillo
Fray Pascual's bulky burlap robe bumps spices into boiling broth
Holy urgency transfigures water into mole
Juan de Palafox y Mendoza
Spain's viceroy
Decreed mole a colonial treasure between steamy mouthfuls

Chichilo
Convent of Santa Rosa's
Impoverished nuns at wit's end
While an Archbishop waits to be fed
Sor Andrea de la Asunción mills stale bits and spice under
divine inspiration
Fragrant sauce poured on wiry turkeys
The sanctified plump gut pleased

Pipián
Long before Cortés sailed into Veracruz
Mōlli simmered in earthen pots
Poured on iguana axolotls acocil
larvae insect-eggs mushrooms
turkey duck dog deer

Negro   Verde   Mancha-manteles
Cosmic Vasconcelian sauce
Drips from Tlaltecuhtli's 9 mouths as
Starved colonial ghosts wander
Thumb beads at dusk and

Whisper ingredient rosaries

cacahuate pasilla pasas pepitas platano
calabasa piñones sal canela
xocolatl ajonjoli oregano
ancho nuez cilantro
comino piña laurel
galleta aceite
clavo ajo.

Ashley La Poeta
By harold terezon

A Ashley la poeta no le gusta la poesía. Si le preguntas ¿porqué? te dirá,
No offense, but poetry is boring.
Si le dices a Ashley la Poeta que te escriba un poema te dirá,

I rather listen to finger nails screeching down a chalkboard than write a poem.
I rather solve a million multiplication problems than write a poem.
I rather smell my cousin's smelly sock while he still has it on than write a poem.
I rather not eat cheese pupusas with curtido for over a month than write a poem.

Pero si le preguntas a Ashley la poeta que te cuente sobre su familia,
se convertirá en un quetzal con alas de arco iris,
su ojos crecerán más grandes que la luna, Júpiter, el sol, ó el universo inmenso,

y te cantará de su hermanita tan bonita y dulce come un fresa pequeñita,
y te cantará de su hermana mayor y su bailes de princesa entres las estrellas,
y te cantará de su papá el disk jockey y su poderes musicales hechos en vinilo de caramelo,
y te cantará de su mamá tan cariñosa como su almohada y cobija favorita.

Y si le dices a Ashley la Poeta que te ha contado un poema sobre su familia
te dirá, *No offense, but that wasn't a poem 'cause poems are boring.*
Y te lo dirá con un sonrisa más grande que un gigante guineo amarillo.

In Case You Forget
By harold terezon

I did not give birth to you
so you could play all day
Oh no
you will not lounge around
like kings & queens of Spain
I don't care how cute & young
you think you are
You will get off your lazy ass
& wash dishes
sweep the kitchen & living room
clean the bathroom
take out the trash
& cut the grass
even if you need scissors
to keep the grass short
You will not get
bad grades at school
because we did not cross borders
risking our lives
so you can chat all day
with your friends
 & come home with a B
I don't care
& I didn't ask how high
you think a B is
You will go to college
You will not consider marriage
or have a boyfriend or girlfriend
until you graduate
Let me remind you that
if I say the sky is green
even if you see it purple
the sky is still green
Just remember
I got the iron's cord
your father's sandals
& a whole lot of olive branches
in the backyard
if you think to say otherwise

& don't think reporting me
to social services
will change a thing
because when I get out of jail
I will come back for you
because there's no way
you will end up like us.

Dear Mr. President
By Maurisa Thompson

Dear Mr. President,

This is a photo of me. I am holding a brown and white cat so that his back legs dangle and his skin wrinkles around his shoulders. But he doesn't seem to mind, he lets me hold him this way. I am eight years old. A newspaper man took this photo when I had been at the stopping house for two days in Chiapas. The people were very kind there, they gave me hugs and messed up my hair the way my uncles and cousins do.

This was two weeks before I arrived in your country. I am not in the newspapers here. The adults here look like police except they stay here all the time, and they yell at us. I count the number of boys in this cell. I don't know how many there are when we are standing up, but it is more crowded when we are lying down. We are waiting for our families to come. I hope my aunt comes soon. Sometimes if we see the guards relax a little, we tell jokes and rhymes and laugh, and we see the stones in their faces soften out of the corner of our eyes. Then some of them yell a little less.

Some of them speak in Spanish the way a bird walks around with one wing broken. I think it would be better if we understood each other. If you let us go to our families, we will be good, we will go to school and learn how to tell stories that make people happy, like cats that let you hold them and trees and other growing things, so that they smile instead of holding their faces still like walls.

Water Crossing
By Maurisa Thompson

where would you go if you had to run?
through the canebrake, machete leaves
that draw less blood than the lash—
run from those that steal children
run, would you *wade in the water*
wade in the water children
god's gonna trouble el agua, las fábricas
pockmarking the land like plantations
the two shirts on your back worth
10 cents per day—
run, on the snake-back of a train
burnish your footprints
from the earth with leaves
from the sand with wool
because they are always behind you
smelling for your blood your body
they would pick from their teeth, run
where would you go to find your mother?
because they think you hold a different god
on your tongue—run from the vice grips
from the armies who twist bayonets in your womb
who forge hells of fire falling from the sky
from bullets that blistered the walls
like tracks of heroin needles on arms
where would you run to?
what possible death
would you choose?
would you dare to ask whatever angels
for safe passage and water to cross
would you set your compass, your eyes
on a star tilting in your vision
and run, run, run, run, run—

and if you could finally stop running
if your heart for a day a week a century
pulled back from throttling your lungs
and rested, and rested, and rested
would you still shroud your own face

would you boil the seas to lethe
clutch guns at the doorway

or would you leave the door open
offer sweet water and maize
to strangers
at your hearth?

Buffalo
By Tara Evonne Trudell

do you
hear me now
screaming
so loud
and scary
not because
I'm crazy
as some
would say
taking emotional
outburst
out of natural
context
last straw falling
breaking my heart
wide open
life tough
all over
me needing
to feel this out
cracking pain
piercing
down deep
hitting spirit
the ache
in my walk
when children
suffer
slow moments
path pausing
pain in heart
containment
I am loud
in my head
at those
around me
not willing
to see

this is not right
this is horrific
as bad as it gets
hell on earth
worse than
purgatory
when children
get caught
in the middle
brown sacrificed
in white politics
everyone
bears witness
not in the best
interest groups
funneling money
into corrupt laws
racist goons
making decisions
for more fools
to follow
opportunity banking
on the migration
of survival
serious profit
the lifetime
of 500 years
killing slow
reducing humanity
treating others
as beneath
nothing
fuck this
patriotic justification
budget concerns
played out
immigration reform
trigger minutemen

racist politicians
corrupt border patrol
worse than
any drug cartel
I can't help
but take a stand
cursing it out
loud in words
necessary
to motivate
people movement
the way
it should be
when children
face danger
alone
my mind racing
with disbelief
trying to keep
a grip
on world realities
what kind of fuckery
is this
when getting away
with murder
is a daily given
bad boy cops
right of passage
making jokes
deciding death
the sick frustrations
of man
continue unnoticed
the acceptance
of people
when in battle
I run
to every corner
handing out
poetry
throwing prayer

beads
at passerby's
wheat-pasting
¡love the refugees!
all over town
taking action
any way
I can
to save
my own child
that one part
of me
I protect
with every breath
my awareness
in raising
chicano power
all my reasons
to fight back
with love
in action
whether
it's yours
hers
or mine
we are
in this together.

c/s

Despedida
By Norma Liliana Valdez

hermano, when you light into tomorrow's dawn
gather a paradise of orchid, a lei of mourning

let loose streams from rivers and blame
the undertow until drought, until desert

until dirt then dust: Texas deep
how fast my thirst succumbed to dusk

night wanted me shadow, wanted me bones
fleshless woman made phantom, all I wanted

was to live, to wield a knife against burials
and die only by truth, briefly gorgeous

the silver quetzal: still ribboned 'round my neck
still tethered to the body and its questions

take me to our distant mountains that I may soar
honeyed earth, color of our mother's hands

free me to mist and volcano, free me
from the words you'll never hear me say

ya llegue hermano, aquí estoy.

Keep 'em Flyin'
By Gloria L. Velasquez

Murió uno de los Greats,
mi compadre José Montoya,
the ultimate chuco que tanto
dio a nuestra gente,
a todos los Louies del barrio,
a todas las Xicanitas que soñaban
con ser poetas como él,
seguir sus pasos y sus consejos
desde Colorado a Califas.

Murío uno de los Greats
Nuestro gran maestro José Montoya,
la voz del Renacimiento Chicano,
el mero mero Piloto de Aztlán
que nunca se olvidó de su Raza
de su pueblo indígena,
de sus raíces humildes.

Adiós, mi querido José
tu comadrita jamás te olvidará,
te llevaré en el cora hasta el día
en que nos encontremos en la gloria
tocando la guitarra y cantando corridos
Ridin' High con el RCAF.

When Women are Trees
by Jeannie Zukav

When Women are Trees
they breathe the world in and out
they know everything and everything knows them.
Every time they speak
life is easy.

When Women are Rain
they leap between the clouds and earth
they know everything and everything knows them.
Every time they soothe the soil
life is easy.

When Women are Lava
they rise up from the center of the world
their blood circulates and creates and creates
they know everything and everything knows them.
Every time their love surges a rhythm
Life is easy.

When Women are Mountains
Mother arms around the world
Stable bones curving into hawk-winged skies
they know everything and everything knows them.
Every time they mediate
life is easy.

When Women are Free
violence fallen away
wisdom healing generations of tyrant fears
They remember everything and everything remembers them.
Every time they laugh
life is easy.